Reading Acquisition in India

RESEARCH IN APPLIED LINGUISTICS

SERIES EDITORS: R.K. AGNIHOTRI AND A.L. KHANNA

Most of the existing theories and models of linguistic analysis have been developed in monolingual societies. When they are applied to multilingual and pluricultural societies, several important aspects of linguistic change are ignored. In fact, the research done in complex multilingual societies has remained so underrepresented that it is not surprising that current linguistic theories have an essentially monolingual orientation.

The primary purpose of this series on Research in Applied Linguistics (RAL) is to present research done in and about multilingual societies such as those of Asia, Africa, Latin America, and the Middle East. An additional aim is to provide a new orientation to the field of Applied Linguistics through careful investigation of the linguistic problems of multilingual societies. Issues of social relevance centering around language will be examined in an interdisciplinary perspective. The series will publish books which have a sound theoretical orientation and carefully documented empirical data.

The following titles have appeared in the series:

1. R.K. Agnihotri and A.L. Khanna (eds), *Second Language Acquisition: Socio-cultural and Linguistic Aspects of English in India* (1994).
2. R.K. Agnihotri and A.L. Khanna (eds), *English Language Teaching in India: Issues and Innovations* (1995).
3. R.K. Agnihotri and A.L. Khanna, *Problematizing English in India* (1997).
4. R.K. Agnihotri, A.L. Khanna and I. Sachdev (eds), *Social Psychological Perspectives on Second Language Learning* (1998).
5. Aditi Mukherjeė and Duggirala Vasanta (eds), *Practice and Research in Literacy* (2002).

READING ACQUISITION IN INDIA

MODELS OF LEARNING AND DYSLEXIA

Research in Applied Linguistics Vol. 6

PURUSHOTTAM G. PATEL

SAGE PUBLICATIONS
New Delhi ■ Thousand Oaks ■ London

First published in 2004 by

Sage Publications India Pvt Ltd
B-42, Panchsheel Enclave
New Delhi 110 017

Sage Publications Inc  **Sage Publications Ltd**
2455 Teller Road 1 Oliver's Yard, 55 City Road
Thousand Oaks, California 91320 London EC1Y 1SP

Published by Tejeshwar Singh for Sage Publications India Pvt Ltd, photo-typeset in 10 pt Calisto MT by Star Compugraphics Private Limited, and printed at Chaman Enterprises, New Delhi.

Library of Congress Cataloging-in-Publication Data

Patel, Purushottam G.
  Reading acquisition in India: models of learning and dyslexia/
Purushottam G. Patel.
    p. cm.—(Research in applied linguistics; v. 6)
  Includes bibliographical references and index.
  1. Dyslexia—India. 2. Reading (Elementary)—Social aspects—India.
  3. Gujarati language—Study and teaching (Elementary). 4. Gujarati
language—Phonology. 5. Brahmi alphabet. I. Title. II. Series.

LB1050.5.P26   491'.4782421—dc22   2004   2004003841

ISBN: 0–7619–3220–8 (US–Hb)   81–7829–349–8 (India–Hb)

Sage Production Team: Sunaina Dalaya, Neeru Handa and
Santosh Rawat

For,

my parents, the late ગરબડભાઈ and ડાહીબેનપટેલ, who gave me everything and asked for nothing in return;

my wife, the late Nandu Patel, who let me grow without obstructing my way for 39 years, 5 months, and 22 days (məmə mənəhə sukhəm bhavəyə!);

and,

my granddaughter, Madison Adelaide Patel (Birdie), who unites us all.

Contents

List of Figures
and Models

LIST OF FIGURES

LIST OF MODELS

Foreword

"The English have no respect for their language," wrote George Bernard Shaw in his preface to *Pygmalion*, "and will not teach their children to speak it. They spell it so abominably that no man can teach himself what it sounds like." Shaw, who wrote *Pygmalion* in 1912, suggests the importance of having better research on phonetics and the importance that should be given to phoneticians so that English orthography can be improved. When Professor Higgins is asked what he is doing, taking notes of the speech of the flower girl, Elijah, and how he deciphers the exact location of the speaker, he explains this science simply as phonetics. He defines this as the science of speech.

In writing this book, Professor Patel not only reemphasizes the value of phonetics (if not of phoneticians) but also of professors of linguistics. Some 90 years after *Pygmalion* was published, the science of speech has acquired roots and runners into neurophysiology, genetics, and the cognitive processes underlying reading. Putting together all of this knowledge into a slim volume is a daunting task. But empirical research in reading acquisition among children in India who are further differentiated in terms of high and low caste, not only requires exquisite planning, but also the courage to attempt binding them together. In consequence, the task of the reader becomes extremely demanding. Reading this volume requires at least a passing knowledge of these fields as well as an openness to learn about the ancient cultural traditions and contemporary practices in India, especially the ill-effects of discrimination arising out of caste prejudices and malnutrition. Professor Patel's major research is in the area of linguistics and reading, the exploration of their relationship to neurophysiology, and only secondarily, the impact on children's reading acquisition in one specific linguistic group in India, which is Gujarati.

Readers who persist in reading the entire book will be delighted to begin learning about the Brāhmī script, which is perhaps the first major script with descendants in a host of South Asian languages. The languages from north and south India are assumed to be so different by the common inhabitants of India, and I count myself as one of them, that not many would be able to imagine a south Indian script with a cousin among all the languages and scripts of northern India. Not only does Brāhmī have descendants in the various scripts of India, but also in countries where Indian culture has impacted the language and literature of South Asian languages like Thai, Burmese, Tibetan, and so on.

If it had come to pass that Professor Higgins, the phonetician, had embraced Sanskrit in the Brāhmī script as the nearest approximation to a phonetically consistent script, and expressed his admiration as such for spoken Sanskrit before Colonel Pickering, Pickering would have disappointed him: "Look Higgins! There are many irregularities in the way a word is written in Brāhmī script, and the way it is spoken and read aloud."[1] Grapheme to phoneme correspondence is vitiated not so much by *matra*, that is the vowel signs that can be attached to

---

[1] The alphabets in the Brāhmī script are organized into vowels and consonants and among the consonants into categories according to their pronunciability. The five categories of consonants are velars (*k, kh, g, gh*), palatals (*th, chh, j, jh*), retroflexes (*p, t, d*), dentals (*e, d*), and lastly, labials (*p* as in pot, and *b*, as in bought).

These well-defined categories of consonants have been supplemented by letters such as *ya, ra,* and *la,* and three kinds of *s* sounds and the *h* sound. The last sound is particularly difficult for the cockney in Shaw's play; Shaw could not bring Elijah to pronounce "hardly," except as "ardly." Bernard Shaw stopped short of combining the talents of Professor Higgins with the knowledge of Sanskrit grammar that Colonel Pickering had, in order to create an ideal writing system.

consonants. Regular words such as *aakuti, maata,* or *patha* are read aloud in consistency with their *matra (maatraa)*, except in the case of a vowel, the guttural *ru.* A simple application of *ru* is found in the word *rushi* (sage). While writing *rushi,* many children and some adult native speakers do use the common consonant *r* rather than the guttural *ru.* Some Sanskrit speakers as well as many speakers of north Indian Sanskrit derivative languages (Oriya, Gujarati, Marathi) will confuse the two, *r* and *ru,* especially when reading a conjoint consonant that has an abbreviated *r* (*krura*=cruel) or an abbreviated *ru (kruta*=made). Also problematic are the *matra* representing some other vowels such as *ai (paitruka),* and *ou,* for example, the words, *mahoushadhi* (great medicine) and *mousumee* (monsoon). Consider also two consonants that have been fused, one dominant and the other present as an abbreviated affix: *priti, prana, purba,* or *prabasee.* In writing these words in Brāhmī-descended scripts such as Oriya, children are alerted to distinguish between *phalaa* (abbreviated secondary consonant), and *maatraa* (abbreviated vowel). *Phalaa* presents extremely difficult orthography in spelling as well as in speech. Consider *wo* and *ya,* the two alphabets that are abbreviated thus: *shwasru* (mother-in-law) and *vaishya* (merchant). The abbreviated *wo* and *ya* have the same *phalaa* (consonant sign) in Oriya, but represent different consonants (*wo* and *ya*)! An added difficulty while writing the word arises in deciding which is the primary and which is the secondary character. Challenge a native speaker of Hindi/Oriya, or Bengali to write the words *shruta* (heard) and *smarana* (remember).

The Brāhmī script may not have fulfilled the requirements of the universal script that Professor Higgins was busy creating, a script that allows a person to teach himself or herself and enable him or her to acquire the right pronunciation. However, it comes close to Shaw's intention of finding a script that is phonetically near-perfect and does not have numerous idiosyncratic ways in which written material can be pronounced.

Orthography in some cases of the Brāhmī script retards reading mainly when conjoint consonants are to be read and spoken. Take for example the words formed exclusively out of the letters, *ba* and *jr*: *ba jra* (thunderbolt). Contrast it with *bra ja* (a village where Lord Krushna lived), *bar ja* abandon, as in *barja niya* (ought to be abandoned). Clearly, the Brāhmī script in reading the *phalaa* may impede children's reading and spelling!

Examples such as these prevent a clean categorization of languages into shallow or deep orthography, the best examples being English and Sanskrit respectively. There are important questions that are raised while identifying possible causes of dyslexia in languages that are shallow or deep. Does the incidence of dyslexia truly depend on orthography? Or are the basic explanations to be found in phonology? Professor Patel could lead us to reflect on these questions and prompt us to suggest if different training programs for reducing reading difficulties in Brāhmī-descended orthographies in contrast to English ought to be considered. The same question has been asked concerning poor reading in English (deep orthography) and Spanish, Italian, and German (shallow orthography). I can give a hint: A remedial reading program that is based on enhancement of (hypothesized) cognitive processes required in reading, PREP, was originally developed for English and has proven to be effective. The program was translated for adoption in Spain (both Castelian and Catalan). What did my Spanish colleagues find? The program showed reading improvement for children who have dyslexia. This is not because as we hypothesized, the cognitive difficulties associated with successive processing (e.g., phonological memory) and simultaneous (verbal–spatial) processing were reduced. These processes are important for reading any script that is based in phonology.

If the reader of this volume finds himself or herself prepared to delve into the intricacies of not only phonology but also explaining reading itself, here he/she will be delighted to find a contemporary, encapsulated review of reading, spelling, and its neuropsychological explanations. The volume's excursion into the cultural habits that surround reading and the abominable instructions given to the so-called scheduled caste children in reading are examined in empirical investigations that will delight the heart of reading researchers. However, the reader must not start feeling inadequate if some parts of the book appear excessively difficult to understand because of a lack of specific knowledge on the part of the reader. I can assure the reader that even for a professional in the related field of psychology and reading, I sometimes had to stop and look up external references in order to understand certain factual paragraphs in this book. As we go through the chapters (don't expect to read it in one sitting) you will find that some parts will make you analyze the meaning of the material and may require intense reflection.

Thus, I conclude as I began: Professor Patel has certainly attempted to integrate several pieces of knowledge, and paint a picture on a broad canvas to not only make the reader more knowledgeable but to also provide an engaging discussion on important issues in many instances.

J.P. Das
University of Alberta
20 June 2003   Edmonton, Canada

Preface and
Acknowledgments

When Donald G. Doehring of McGill University invited me to join him in his research project on "specific reading disability" in 1975, I was interested in the cognitive–neural–linguistic developmental changes in children between five and seven years of age. I instantly began integrating psycholinguistics with neuropsychology, specifically to understand developmental dyslexia in the context of the emergence of reading in language development. With Don Doehring I found a footing in the domain of developmental dyslexia and component skills in reading acquisition.

When I read Rutter, Tizard, and Whitmore's 1970 book *Education, Health and Behaviour*, I decided to spend a month at the Institute of Psychiatry in London where I read a great deal about "otherwise normal children" and "cycles of disadvantage" (Rutter and Madge, 1976). Then came a beautiful interlude at Camarillo State Hospital and the University of California at Los Angeles, with Paul Satz and his postdoctoral fellows in whose company I got an opportunity to learn more about language, cognition, and the brain within the framework of developmental neuropsychology. This was a major step in my understanding of developmental dyslexia.

In 1983, I returned to India to do research on reading acquisition in Gujarati supported by a faculty research fellowship from the Shastri Indo-Canadian Institute. During my stay in Vadodara, Dr. Bharati Modi asked me to read her thesis on the Gujarati sound system, which introduced me to the ancient Indian *Pratishakhya* literature for the first time. She also gave me D.D. Mahulkar's monograph *The Pratishakhya Tradition and Modern Linguistics*, a most appropriate present for me at the time.

In 1990, I ran into David Barton in Thessaloniki-Halkidiki. In the context of the controversy regarding the cognitive consequences of (alphabetic) literacy for societies, David asked me a simple question: "Was Panini, the father of modern linguistics, illiterate?" The issue about orality, literacy, and creative scholarship in ancient India vis-à-vis the claims put forward by Eric Havelock, Jack Goody, and David R. Olson developed into a research proposal. The Shastri Indo-Canadian Institute, in 1992, again awarded a faculty research fellowship to enable me to spend six months in India. It was in this context that I began to understand oral composition, oral learning, the recitation of Vedic literature, and the development of the brāhmī script in India.

At an Indian classical music concert, I sat next to Bharati Modi who drew my attention to the musician's performance of *vikruti* which involves manipulating the seven notes, *sa, re, ga, ma, pa, dha, ni* into different arrangements. The next morning I found Abhyankar and Devasthali's (1978) book on *vikruti*, which opened many more doors into the process of the Vedic oral tradition. While delving into the mechanics of unit re-organization in *vikruti*, the oral composition of metrical verses, and the practice of recitation, I became fascinated by the linguistic design of the brāhmī script and the concept of *akṣara*, both as a spoken and a written unit. It was at this time that I met Baljit Kaur who showed me how the different Brāhmī scripts worked and asked me about the linguistic underpinnings of the concept of *matra*, which turned out to be a central question in my work.

In 1996, I entered the competition for the third time for an award from the Shastri Indo-Canadian Institute to go to Vadodara to collect more data on reading acquisition among Gujarati children. In 1983, I focused only on the children from mainstream groups in a private school. At the beginning of the 1997 project in Vadodara, I stumbled upon public schools* which were mainly attended by children whose

---

* By "public schools" the author means "government schools" here and in the rest of the book.

parents belonged to the "scheduled" castes and tribes and lived, essentially, on the outskirts of mainstream Hindu society; I referred to this group as "disadvantaged children from scheduled groups." I was intrigued by what I found. In 1999, I managed to get a minor grant from the Canadian International Development Research Agency. This time, I accidentally discovered a public school for girls whose parents belonged to the scheduled groups and lived in an upper-class residential area. In spite of their socioeconomic disadvantages, these girls were regular in attendance and showed exceptionally positive motivation. I referred to them as "advantaged children from scheduled groups from mainstream outbuildings" and treated them as a natural experimental group.

I have given this personal account in order to identify those individuals and institutions to whom I owe so much. I am indebted to the Shastri Indo-Canadian Institute for three Faculty Research Fellowship Awards. Also important was the research-intensive sabbatical system at the University of Ottawa, which facilitated my trips to India.

I have had the privileged access to Joseph F. Kess' (University of Victoria) phenomenal scholarly background, experience in book writing, and a genuine sense of friendship. Joe read the entire manuscript line by line and made many valuable suggestions regarding the concerns of the prospective reader. Also most helpful was Melanie Sellar who has an exceptional editorial talent, an acutely perceptive mind and an excellent background in cognitive science. At the end, I asked Ann Stuart Laubstein to put her discerning, analytical, and sedulous mind to work. In spite of all of her other obligations and plans, Ann scoured the manuscript precisely the way I wanted and made lots of observations which improved both the content and the style. Ann's expertise in psycholinguistics and phonology forced me to rethink some relevant issues.

Among my peers in research on reading acquisition in India, Ajit Mohanty of Utkal University and P. Prakash of Mysore University, have been exceptionally warm and generous hosts. Ajit organized a symposium, which gave me an opportunity to interact with Pratibha Karanth and D. Vasanta. Prakash gave me a tutorial on his own research projects and helped me to deepen my understanding of the way the Kannada script encodes words. He also read an early version of the manuscript and made encouraging comments. Both Ajit and Prakash offered their observations about the ongoing sociolinguistic change regarding the schwa in Oriya and Kannada speech patterns, respectively.

At the M.S. University of Baroda, Neema Ghadia, a native speaker of Gujarati and a linguist, served as a research assistant and helped me in the preparation of test materials and data collection in 1997 and 1999. Neema gave me the Gujarati speech games, which she knew and had used in verbal play as a child. Dilip Rajgor showed me how to read the Ashokan Brāhmī script and Pramod Pandey shared his expertise in phonology, and welcomed me into his family. Later, Pramod read the manuscript and made some useful suggestions.

At a different level, I owe an enormous debt to two individuals in Vadodara: Bela Desai and her entire family demonstrated the practice of Indian hospitality at its best. In the same spirit, Kalindi Nanavaty allowed me the use of the guest room in her flat and nourished me with her tasty and nutritional cooking for more than three months.

At the University of Ottawa, my two colleagues, Phil C. Hauptman and Ian Mackay, have readily helped whenever I was inadequate in computer literacy. Enrique Astorga came to my rescue with cheerful generosity whenever I needed help in managing my computer. Without the timely help of Dawn Harvie, who knows how to make computers behave, the tables would have definitely looked baggy.

I am also happy to acknowledge the contributions of my three sons. When I started wearing two parental hats after 12 November 2001 when Nandu reached *parinirvana*, Kint got interested in what dad was doing. He combed the manuscript and made several suggestions. I knew that he was a talented writer, but I didn't know that he was such a skilled editor. Kint also expressed a desire to create a cover for the book. Ben and Chuck and their life partners, Heidi and Treena respectively, are also the most caring and supporting keepers of my soul. Chuck and Treena's dog Indy is an equal partner in the family enterprise.

Finally, I should like to thank my editor at Sage, Sunaina Dalaya, for her editorial competence and personal grace. Sunaina's precise queries clearly indicated that she grasped the content of the book and her interaction with the author was civilized.

Introduction

In literate societies, most children learn to read as naturally as they begin to speak and systematically mature in language development. Around the age of five weeks, babies turn crying into a code of communication. The family and the speech community provide social–cultural–linguistic routines, which help the babies to develop the cry into language. Subsequently, the child gains exposure to printed language in the environment and the process of reading acquisition emerges. In schools, this process of learning to read further strengthens and children begin to read in order to learn.

India's Ancient Oral Tradition

India's ancient oral tradition provides a particularly relevant stimulus to beginning reading, especially related to the rise of awareness about timing units and patterns in speech. Children experience a great deal of oral learning and poetic recitation, which help them to break up words into syllabic and subsyllabic timing units. The poems they memorize and the recitations they hear are composed in rhythmically organized rising, falling, and elongated patterns of accentuation. What is known as "phonological" awareness in the research literature on reading acquisition is fostered in a natural way by the Vedic oral tradition. In the current models based on alphabetic acquisition, the ability to recognize and manipulate subword units like the syllable and the phoneme is considered to be pivotal in learning to read.

LINGUISTIC DESIGN OF BRĀHMĪ

The linguistic design of the scripts used by most of the Indo-Aryan and Dravidian languages has roots in the ancient Indian script known as Brāhmī. The development of the Brāhmī orthographic unit *akṣara* was influenced by the new language sciences, namely, phonetics, metres, and grammar. At the basis of the orthographic unit *akṣara* was the concept of *matra*. The Indian concept of *matra* is based upon syllable quantity and corresponds to the modern term mora. While length is a property of vowels, quantity is a property of syllable structure. As Allen (1987, p. 105) points out, the ancient Hindu grammarians "used the terms long and short to apply to vowel-length, but heavy and light to apply to syllable quantity." The syllable ending with a consonant or a consonant cluster is heavy in quantity; for example, cvc or vc is heavy in quantity. On the other hand, syllables with short vowels with or without a preceding consonant or a consonant cluster, and more importantly, no consonant or consonant cluster at the end, are considered light in quantity.

THE *akṣara* AS A WRITTEN UNIT

The *akṣara*s encode cv, cvv, ccv, ccvv, cccv, cccvv, v, and vv. Note that vv stands for a long vowel or a diphthong, and not two vowels. The obvious question is about the fate of the postvocalic consonants in syllables: Postvocalic consonants with certain features form *akṣara*s, while the others are integrated with the following *akṣara*s. The *akṣara*s in words which contain cvc, cvcc, and vc syllable structures are formed on the basis of the *matra* value of a given postvocalic consonant:

Consonants which approximate the *matra*, that is, the duration value of a short vowel form *akṣərə*s, while the other consonants move on to the following syllable in the word. When the final consonant in cvc approximates the duration value of a whole *matra*, it appears to give rise to a juncture. It is accepted in phonetics that consonants before vowels in syllables are short and phonologists suggest that the onset consonants have no prosodic value. On the other hand, postvocalic consonants in syllables can be either short or long; in other words, only the postvocalic consonants can be assigned a *matra* value. Look at the following examples:

syllables	*akṣərə*s	word	gloss
cvv cvv	cvv cvv	*māyā*	attachment
cvc cv	cv c cv	*batli*	bottle
cvvc cvv	cvv ccvv	*mātrā*	mora
cvc cv	cv c cv	*bəkri*	female goat
cvc cvc	cv ccv c	*ḍuʃmən*	enemy
cv cvc	cv cv c	*chakər*	servant
cvc cv	cv c cv	*matli*	clay pot

The principles underlying *akṣərə* formation speak directly to the different models of syllable structure in current phonological theory. The rules of *akṣərə* formation favor some models and reject the approach which considers the unit called rime, which is a combination of the vocalic nucleus and the following consonant, a natural bond (Kiparsky, 1979). The *akṣərə*s are combinations of the onset and the vocalic nucleus. Also interesting, theoretically, is the treatment of the word-internal and word-final consonants in *akṣərə* formation.

LANGUAGE SCIENCE IN ANCIENT INDIA

There is a general consensus that language science originated and matured in ancient India (Allen, 1953; Mahulkar, 1981, 1990; Varma, 1961). There is also no doubt that Brāhmī was developed in India several centuries before the beginning of the Christian Era (Gupta and Ramachandran, 1979). However, the systematic use of writing in Brāhmī was scarce until the 1st century of the Christian Era when the Buddhist monks in Sri Lanka began writing down the so far orally composed and transmitted teachings of Buddha. The practice of oral composition, learning, and recitation, though mainly restricted to the priestly caste, influences the learning system as a whole and permeates all walks of life amongst the Hindu people. The popular musical programs like "Sa Re Ga Ma Pa" and "Antakshari" on Indian television at present bode well for the oral tradition. People from different age groups and occupations sing film as well as classical songs on the basis of oral memory. All the religious and social ceremonies in Hindu society are melodius.

The culture of the oral tradition is a part of the developmental course for mainstream Hindu children. The same advantages of the Vedic oral tradition are not fully accessible to children of the scheduled groups who also experience the culture of poverty, the stigma of low socioeconomic status, and horrendous environmental toxicants. The label "scheduled" identifies members of the tribes and low castes who are given compensatory advantages. The question of reading acquisition in these children who mainly attend public school, involves a different set of issues and challenges in remedial instruction.

READING ACQUISITION AND CHILD LITERACY IN INDIA

Any perspective on reading acquisition in India also cannot ignore the slow historical growth of functional literacy through the 20th century. What happened before the beginning of the modern era is a matter of a simple guess. Since only practicing Brahmins (the caste associated with learning and religious ceremonies) and a handful of others involved in administration and trade attempted to acquire literacy, the masses treated the printed word as something mysterious. As a matter of general practice, the link between written language and the ordinary people was indirect, that is, mediated by only a few literate individuals.

The literacy figures between 1901 and 1931 cited by Parulekar (1939) are compelling. The percentage of literate people in India for 1901, 1911, 1921, and 1931 was 5.3, 5.4, 6.3, and 6.9 respectively. Between 1901 and 1931, the rise in literacy was less than 1 percent per decade. However, there is a change in the growth pattern in terms of males and females in urban and rural areas after India achieved independence. Table 1 shows growth rate of literacy in India, in percentage, from 1951 to 1991.

Table 1
Literacy Growth in India, 1951–91

	1951	1961	1971	1981	1991
Total	18.3	28.3	34.4	41.4	52.2
Males	27.2	40.4	45.9	53.4	64.2
Females	8.9	15.3	22.0	28.5	39.2

Source: Statistics from Centre for Monitoring Indian Economy, 1994.

The implication of these figures is clear: When most children are learning to read, they are surrounded by adult relatives, who are either illiterate or preliterate. Obviously, these adults do not read and write; therefore, they are forced to speak mainly about the "here and now" matters which are related to very limited contexts. In some way, this must obstruct the cognitive–linguistic development in these children.

What compels attention in the Indian situation is the dropout rate for grade school children from the Scheduled Castes and the Scheduled Tribes. For the academic year 1989–90, the dropout rates for grades one to four were as follows:

Total	48.08
Scheduled Castes	50.32
Scheduled Tribes	66.66

Daswani presents a telling picture of child literacy in India in the following:

> There are nearly 170 million children between six and fourteen years of age, but only about 90 million of them attend primary school. Most children who enter grade 1 of the formal school do not complete the five years of the primary stage. Only about a quarter of the children who enter primary school go on to the next stage, upper primary school. The primary and the upper primary stages together make up the stipulated eight years of elementary education promised to all children in India (1999, p. 435).

The Question of Dyslexia in Poor/Scheduled Caste Children

The nature of the difficulties faced by these poor children in India in reading acquisition presents a problem for research in developmental dyslexia, especially in terms of methodology. Due to the focus on the neural–cognitive deficits in dyslexia in otherwise normal children, the children with poverty, low intelligence, and lack of opportunities are excluded from research studies (Eisenberg, 1978; Rutter, 1978). Researchers argue that the findings on dyslexic type of reading in poor children cannot be unambiguously attributed to neurobiological–cognitive deficits. The possibility that extreme poverty, environmental hazards, and socio–cultural–religious shame can cause dyslexic-type neurobiological damage has so far been ignored. This methodological requirement gave rise to the myth of the otherwise normal middle-class dyslexic child (Eisenberg, 1978).

Late Arrival of Printing in India

Also noteworthy is the late arrival of book printing in India (Kesavan, 1988). The first printing press was established in Goa in 1556, thanks to the Jesuit missionaries from Portugal who published, in 1557, the book *Doctrina Christa* by St. Xavier. Chennai saw its first printing press in 1712: Danish missionaries printed the book *Damulian Tongue*. Mumbai had to wait until 1780 to print *Calendar for the Year of Our Lord* and the first book appeared in 1793 in English (Priolkar, 1958). Even if the printing press had arrived earlier, it probably would not have made any significant difference. The Rgvedic hymns were not edited and written down until the second half of the 14th century; prior to that they were kept in memory and kept alive by the practice of recitation. To add to it all, Pereira (1999) complains in a newspaper article that, in general, literate Indians do not read on a regular basis.

My focus on the phonological design of the ǝkṣǝrǝ is not intended to suggest that learning to read is all about decoding and phonics. The child learns to read to enter the literate world and acquires information in different domains, for example, herbs, genetics, and ancient civilizations. She might also enjoy reading Rabindranath Tagore. She might also be required to read a letter or the epics Ramayana and Mahabharata to an illiterate grandmother or a neighbor, which would require her to read orally, that is, to transform orthography into speech.

My approach involves a framework which cross-fertilizes phonology, psycholinguistics, cognitive neuroscience, and "anthropology of literacy." As for the logic and heuristics of research methodology, I am in tune with Rubin (1989): "less control of the experimental conditions and less control of the responses the subjects are allowed to make"(p. 86). I also follow Rubin's guideline to avoid strict adherence "to any one theory or hypothesis when starting to collect data."

Given here are some Sanskrit terms in phonetic transcription. The straight line over the vowel letters indicates length. For example, *mātra* = *maatraa*. In the text, vowel length in ǝkṣǝrǝ formation is indicated by vv; that is, vv = v: (a long vowel or a diphthong). The phonetic symbol [ǝ] represents the mid-central vowel known as schwa, which is pronounced like *a* in ǝkṣǝrǝ, in Sanskrit, Hindi, and Gujarati.

Roman	Phonetic
ǝkṣǝrǝ	ǝkṣǝrǝ
anusvara	ǝnusvārǝ
Brahmi	brāhmī
matra	mātrā
Panini	pāṇini
Pratishakhya	prātiʃākhya
Rgved	r̥gved
Shakalya	ʃakǝlyǝ
varnamala	vǝrṇamālā

Chapter One

WRITING SYSTEMS, SCRIPTS, AND ORTHOGRAPHIES

INTRODUCTION

The terms "writing system," "script," and "orthography" pervade the scholarly literature on written language and literacy (Coulmas, 1996). These terms are used in specific contexts and it is therefore necessary to specify these. Many researchers use the terms "language" and "script" interchangeably, which is clearly misleading; often you will come across statements like "The English language is alphabetic, while the Japanese language is syllabic." No language is alphabetic or syllabic. It is simply a case of the structural properties of some languages being suitable to certain types of scripts. For example, the sound structure of the Chinese language is such that it is difficult to match it with the Roman script, which is a mixture of alphabetic, syllabic, and morphemic units. Similarly, Japanese syllables (*a*, *ki*, *ra*, *o*, *ta*, and so on) are suited to the syllabic, or more appropriately, moraic mode. The use of the terms phonemic, syllabic, and morphemic is also inappropriate. In the context of this book, most researchers refer to Indian scripts as syllabic or semi-syllabic, which is not the case.

Language can be used through the medium of speech, writing, or signs. Speech represents language in terms of utterances with correlate prosodic patterns. Utterances involve semantic–syntactic categories and relations, which are carried by words. Words are made up of morphemes, syllables, and still smaller subsyllabic units.

The morpheme connects lexical and relational meaning with grammatical and word formation processes. Those that stand for lexical meaning are called lexemes or content morphemes. The grammatical morphemes connect meaning with the grammatical system through what traditional grammar calls affixes (prefixes, infixes, and suffixes). The grammatical morphemes also include entities, which are not affixed to words, like prepositions, conjunctions, conditionals and quantifiers in English. The derivational morphemes introduce changes, which allow derivation of one grammatical class from the other, as in "active" and "actor" from "act." Logical categories, which are dealt with in symbolic or mathematical logic, like conjunctions (and, but), quantifiers (some, any), negatives (no, not, none), conditional (if, if and only if), etc., are also grammatical morphemes.

The syllable is a meaningless speech unit involving a vowel or a syllabic consonant, often a sonorant, which may be preceded and/or followed by a consonant or a consonant cluster. The consonant or consonant cluster preceding the vowel is called the "onset" and the consonant following the vowel is called the "coda." The vowel is known as the "nucleus" or "peak." The nucleus involves a short vowel or a long vowel or a diphthong. The combination of the onset and the nucleus is referred to as "body"; while the combination of the nucleus and the coda is referred to as "rime." The prosodic values of the consonants in the onset and the coda positions are different. The onset consonants are supposed to play no role in the quantity value of the syllable, while the coda consonants do. The traditional distinctions between "closed" and "open" and "light" and "heavy" syllables depends upon the presence or absence of the end consonants: The presence of postvocalic consonants makes the syllables "closed" and "heavy." Put simply, open syllables end in vowels, while closed syllables end in consonants. For example, cv, cc, cccv, cvv, ccvv, cccvv are open syllables and vc, vvc, cvc, vc, etc., are closed syllables.

While speech is carried by sound waves, writing is transmitted through scripts. Some scripts encode the conceptual content of morphemes, which is the characteristic of Chinese writing. Some scripts represent the mora, which is a meaningless sound unit with marked acoustic properties, which is the case of the Japanese syllabary known as kana. The Japanese writing system involves two types—a lexemic Chinese kanji and a syllabic kana (see Kess and Miyamoto, 1999 for a comprehensive and scholarly treatment of the different writing systems in Japan). The alphabetic system mainly represents all the subsyllabic components, that is, the onset, the nucleus, and the coda. In varying degrees, the different alphabets use morphemes and syllables as well.

The different scripts derived from the ancient Indian script known as Brāhmī present an interesting case. The linguistic design of Brāhmī is based upon the principle of breaking up the syllable into two components, keeping the vowel and the preceding consonant or consonant cluster together as a unit. The consonant or consonant cluster after the vowel in syllables is treated differently. The Indian phoneticians recognized the distinction between syllabic quantity and vowel length. Later, the Greek phoneticians also recognized this distinction and established a convention: The short vowel was taken as a "primary measure of time" which was known as "kronos protos"; hence, a long vowel or a diphthong was valued as two short vowels, while a consonant was valued as a half-short vowel (Allen, 1981, p. 122). The ancient Indian phoneticians, on the other hand, clarified and specified the distinction between vowel length and syllable quantity in terms of the *matra* as a basic unit of syllabic quantity:

short vowel = one *matra*
long vowel = two *matras*
diphthong = two *matras*
short consonant = half *matra*
long consonant = one *matra*

The corresponding term for *matra* in Latin is mora, which is taken as a timing unit in music and modern linguistics. While the sequences are segmented into rhythmic units carrying equal time in music, the prosody of utterances is marked by timing units, which correspond to a short vowel with or without preceding consonants.

The orthographic unit *akṣarə* represents *matra* values. Hence, the *akṣarə* in Brāhmī scripts can encode cv, ccv, cccv, v, vv, cvv, ccvv, cccvv, and c (long consonant following the nucleus). Here vv stands for a long vowel or a diphthong. The Brāhmī script divides syllables into (consonants) + vowels and consonants: The consonant(s) before the vowel(s) are kept, but the consonants after the vowels are treated differently. Look at the following examples showing syllable and *akṣarə* composition:

syllable	*akṣarə*	
cv	cv	
cvc	cv	c
ccvc	ccv	c
v	v	
vv	vv	
ccccvvc	cccvv	c

Writing systems are labelled according to the linguistic unit that is typically represented in script topography. The Chinese character represents the morpheme and, in some cases, clues about how it may be understood and pronounced. The Chinese system is lexigraphic, as it encodes lexemes, the morphemes with a semantic basis. This is called logography, as Chinese words mainly consist of single morphemes, which are word stems. Chinese also has lots of compounds. Japanese also uses this system to represent the stems of words. However, Japanese words involve stems and grammatical prefixes and suffixes, which can be represented as morae. Hence, the Japanese writing system consists of lexigraphic kanji (derived from the Chinese Hanzi) and moraic kana (see Kess and Miyamoto, 1999 for a detailed analysis of the case of Japanese in relation to Chinese). Alphabetic writing implies a grapheme to phoneme conversion system. The Finnish alphabet is an ideal example, while English and French are mixed systems, that is, they also allow letter groups, which correspond to morphemes and syllables.

The term orthography applies to the standard way in which the different linguistic units are represented in a given writing system. It involves rules of representation, that is, how written units correspond to spoken units, such as, phonemes, morae, syllables, and morphemes. For example, in English, which uses the alphabetic Roman script, the word *action* has two morphemes: *act* and *tion*. The first morpheme *act* is represented by three phonemes, *a, k,* and *t,* while *tion* stands for the second morpheme as a whole without distinct phonemic correspondences. Orthographic rules also include the use of punctuation.

The current models of alphabetic reading acquisition are motivated in terms of the hypothesis that the child at the doorstep of literacy needs to be aware that words are made up of sound units, namely, syllables and phonemes. Several research teams have explored the hypothesis that awareness about the segmental basis of linguistic units in speech might be an essential first step in reading acquisition. Which linguistic unit plays a critical role in beginning to read is a crucial question in current research on reading acquisition in the West (Goswami and Bryant, 1990; Gough et al., 1992). The linguistic organization of the script and its cultural context are hardly taken into account in research motivated in terms of competing models.

Given a linguistically designed script and the background of an ancient tradition of oral learning, India provides an interesting field for the study of language, script, orthography, and literacy. The speech communities in the subcontinent use a large number of languages which belong to different genetic families. Hindi, Bengali, and Punjabi, for example, belong to the Indo-European family with historical ties to English, French, and Persian, among others. Tamil, Telugu, Kannada, and Malayalam are among the languages belonging to the Dravidian family. Table 1.1 lists the language families in India; Table 1.2 lists those languages in modern India which use the Brāhmī script.

Table 1.1
Language Families in India

Indo-Aryan	Assamese
	Bengali
	Gujarati
	Hindi
	Marathi
	Oriya
	Punjabi
	Sindhi

(Table 1.1 continued)

(Table 1.1 continued)

Dardic	Kashmiri
Dravidian	Kannada
	Malayalam
	Tamil
	Telugu
Austro-Asiatic	
Munda	Ho
	Santali
Mon-Khmer	Khasi
Tibeto-Burman	Garo

Table 1.2
Languages in Modern India Using Brāhmī Scripts

Dravidian	Tamil
	Malayalam
	Kannada
	Telugu
Indo-Aryan	Hindi (Devanagari Script)
	Marathi
	Gujarati
	Punjabi (Gurumukhi Script)
	Kashmiri (Sharada/Devanagari Scripts)
	Bengali
	Assamese
	Oriya
	Sindhi (Devanagari)
	Konkani (Marathi, Kannada, Roman)

Chapter Two

ANCIENT INDIAN CULTURAL–LINGUISTIC HERITAGE

INTRODUCTION

Every culture, literate or preliterate, has a repertoire of verbal rituals and routines, albeit in varying degrees. The maturing child brain takes this as a source of stimulation for cultural–psycholinguistic development. The different types of verbal involvement are likely to foster the ability to perceive and manipulate the syllabic and subsyllabic units. The English speech games like Pig Latin, Ubby Dubby, Toppy Hoppy, riddles, moron jokes, and nursery rhymes provide such a linguistic ecology (Patel, 1983). In India, the situation is unique; this type of verbal ecology is rooted in the ancient oral tradition. Literary composition centered around syllabic quantity, which governed the different types of metrical arrangement. The same unit of syllabic quantity was used to form *akṣaras* (orthographic units) when the script known as Brāhmī was developed (if not invented).

The earliest literary creations of India, the Vedas, and the scholarly and philosophical works following them, were composed orally and for centuries transmitted as such. To maintain oral learning and storage, the process of speech production was studied, which in my view was the beginning of speech science, in particular, and linguistics, in general. Of particular importance are the methods of recitation and the different types of text and metrical arrangements (Patel, 1996). The subsyllabic unit, *matra*, was taken as a timing unit, the duration of which can be shortened or lengthened to create melodic meters. The text was decomposed and arranged in different ways known as *patha*s and *vikruti*s. The word *vikruti* means "deformation"; the process involved subsyllabic segmentation, ˙rearrangement of these units, and their synthesis, which involved morphemic, syllabic, and phonemic units.

The terms *pada* and *patha* warrant a brief explanation. While *matra* was a basic unit of syllabic quantity, that is, duration, the term *patha* was created to deal with the level which connects *matra*s to grammar and meaning. According to Abhyankar and Shukla's (1986, p. 233) *A Dictionary of Sanskrit Grammar*, the term *pada* was originally applied to the individual words, which constituted the Vedic *samhita* text, that is, the continuous text that was recited. Panini's definition of *pada* included complete noun-forms and verb-forms as well as prefixes and suffixes. The units were marked by two types of pauses: *danda* (longer duration) and *avagraha* (shorter duration). According to Jha (1987, p. 13),

> danda represents intervention by the length of time required to pronounce a short vowel (ekamatra—'one matra') between the two finished words; whereas, an avagraha represents the intervention by the length of time required to pronounce a consonant (ardhamatra—'half matra') between two phonological units.

The concept of *patha* played a crucial role in the way the original text was segmented and reorganized for recitation and oral learning. The continuous text known as *samhitapatha* was transformed into a segmented text known as *padapatha* by Shakalya, the first truly gifted linguist whom Panini recognized as a worthy predecessor. The creation of *padapatha* required a mastery of morphophonemics in Vedic Sanskrit, that is, the changes that take place when the sounds at the edges of the adjoining morphemes are joined. This process is known as *sandhi*, which constitutes well-defined rules. The creation of the *kramapatha* is a much more complicated process. The best authoritative source for the different types of *vikruti* with formation rules and illustrations is K.V. Abhyankar and G.V. Devasthali's 1978 monograph, *Veda-Vikruti-Lakshana-Samgraha.*

For our purpose, we will take a simple example from an article on *kramapatha* by Devasthali (1978, p. 575), who is an acknowledged authority on the topic:

samhita	वाजेषु सासहिर्भव
səmhita	vajeṣu sasəhirbhəvə
pada	वाजेषु| ससहिः	भव|
padə	vajeṣu/sasəhi:/bhəvə/
krama	वाजेषु सासहिः	सासहिर्भव|
krəmə	vajeṣu sasəhi:/sasəhi:rbhəvə/

The derivatives of the *padapatha* and *kramapatha* were called *vikruti*s, which were also performed orally for recitation. In the *kramapatha*, the arrangement is ab, bc, cd, de, while in the type of *vikruti* called *jata* (braid), the order of the *pada*s is /abbaab/bccbbc/cddccd/deedde/ and in the *vikruti ghana* (bell), the sequence is /abbaabccbaac/ bccbbcddcbbcd/cddccdeedccde/. The *vikruti*s *mala* (garland), *shikha* (topknot), and *rekha* (row), among others, were much more complicated.

The tradition of Vedic recitation in *samhitapatha*, *padapatha*, *kramapatha*, and the *patha*s in several *vikruti*s is alive in present-day India in specific areas.

The ancient Indian literature was composed in different types of metrical arrangement. Pandits recited them frequently on occasions which were the core of religious–cultural routines. The practice of recitation exists in varying degrees in the various geographic–linguistic regions in present-day India. What is striking is that folk songs, wedding songs, lullabies, and children's poetry in contemporary India follow the ancient metrical tradition which accentuates the əkṣərə in the rising, falling, and continued patterns.

What is relevant to the issue of psycholinguistic development, in general, and segmental awareness, in particular, is that children in

India are allowed to attend almost all the religious, cultural, and social events. Children get attuned to the metrical arrangements at these events, which are so common in the Hindu way of life. This practice is enhanced and systematized in schools where they are required to memorize poems and arithmetic tables, and recite them regularly as part of the curriculum. All these religious–social–cultural and schooling routines foster psycholinguistic development, especially sound unit awareness, which is associated with the emergence of literacy in early childhood.

Except for the Roman alphabetic and the Perso-Arabic scripts, as previously mentioned, the scripts used in India are offshoots of a script developed in ancient India around the 7th century B.C., namely, Brāhmī (Upasak, 1960; Verma, 1971). Whatever the origin of the initial form of Brāhmī may be, there is no doubt that its sophisticated linguistic design was worked out by the ancient Hindu scholar(s) to represent the sound structure of Prakrit and Sanskrit. The phonological principle underlying the Brāhmī orthographic unit known as the *akṣarə* is still functional in its derivative scripts like Devanagari, Tamil, Kannada, Telugu, Malayalam, Bengali, Oriya, Gurumukhi, and Gujarati. The historical changes involve mainly topographic details in visuospatial organization.

USE OF WRITING IN ANCIENT INDIA

The question of writing in ancient India has interesting implications (Patel, 1996). The use of writing in India dates back to 2550–1900 B.C., the time period of the Indus Valley people who lived in India before the Rgvedic Indo-Aryans. The Indus Valley people, whose linguistic–racial origin is unknown, were literate and used writing. There is no consensus about the type of writing system and the language used by these people. The issue of the use of writing in India after the end of the Indus Valley Civilization is interesting, because the first appearance of Brāhmī in India is seen only in the Ashokan inscriptions, which belong to the 3rd century before the beginning of the Christian Era. These inscriptions were written in Brāhmī and Kharoṣti. Brāhmī flourished and gave rise to the modern Indic scripts, while Kharoṣti prevailed in India only during the 3rd century B.C. to the 3rd century A.D.

The Rgvedic people, who are supposed to have followed the Indus Valley people, were pastoral and preliterate. They were indeed exceptionally creative and scholarly people, but they preferred the oral mode of learning and composition. There is a consensus that there is no clearly interpretable reference to writing in Vedic literature. It can be reasonably assumed that writing as a means of recording information was known, but it was used mainly to mark objects and not to record literature and science.

The issue of the practice of writing during Vedic India is considered in Oza's (1918) influential publication written in Hindi. Pandit Oza suggests that the Vedic scholars must have used writing, but the manuscripts written by them could not survive, as the materials for writing used at the time were perishable.

It has also been suggested that specific stanzas in the Rgveda allude to writing, in that they refer to language that is heard and language that is seen. Also a line in the 10th section of the Rgveda (10. 62. 7) mentions that King Savarni gave away 1,000 cows with the number eight marked on the ears of each. Similarly, the mention of the names of several meters like *gayatri*, *anushtubh*, *brihati*, and *jagati* as well as the numeric figures like *dasa* (ten), *sata* (hundred), *sahasra* (thousand), *nyuta* (hundred thousand), and so on, is also considered relevant evidence indicating the use of writing at the time. This suggestion assumes that the mechanics of poetic meters and the use of complex numbers cannot exist without the systematic use of writing.

The maturity and sophistication of the linguistic understanding necessary for the creation of Rgveda *padapatha*, Rgveda *kramapatha*, and the different *vikrutis*, it seems, preceded the creation of Brāhmī. The first known appearance of the use of Brāhmī is the inscriptions engraved on the rocks, pillars, and slabs which belong to the period starting from the middle of the 3rd century B.C., specifically to Emperor Ashoka (269–232 B.C.). As Upasak (1960, p. 21) suggests, Brāhmī

> may have begun as a mercantile alphabet, based either on vague memories of the Harrapan script or derived from contact with Semitic traders, or indeed it may have owed something to both these sources; but by the time of Ashoka, it was the most developed scientific script of the world.

To see how Brāhmī emerged from under the shadow of the practice of oral learning and recitation, which may have given impetus to the genesis of language science, I will try to paint, with a speculative brush, a possible scenario of what might have happened in ancient India (Patel, 1996, p. 322), in Model 2.1.

Model 2.1
Cultural–Linguistic Developmental Contexts of Brāhmī

Literate Indus Valley Civilization
Pastoral Vedic Society: Oral Composition and Learning: *Rgveda Samhita*   *Shakalya's Rgved Padapatha*   *Rgveda Kramapatha*   *Vikrutis*
Saunaka's Rgveda Pratishakhya   *Yaska's Nirukta*   *Panini's Aṣṭadhyāyī*
Brāhmī
Emperor Ashoka's Inscriptions in Brāhmī

The linguistic design of Brāhmī, and its scarce use before Emperor Ashoka's time suggests that what happened in India is in contrast to the events that took place in ancient Greece. In Greece, the science of language followed the development of the alphabet. The Phoenician consonantal system was improvised to add vowel signs, which were necessary to represent the Greek sound system. On the other hand, Brāhmī owes its linguistic design to the ancient Indian science of phonetics. Staal (1975, p. 341) rightly suggests that "in India, meta-linguistic notions originated early, and a phonetic system of writing was adopted later. By the time that a phonetic writing was adopted in India, the linguistic analysis of the language was already well advanced."

Chapter Three

SOME LINGUISTIC FEATURES OF BRĀHMĪ SCRIPTS

INTRODUCTION

Brāhmī was originally used to write Prakrit, a derivative of Sanskrit; Sanskrit was written in Brāhmī four centuries later. The sacred religious texts were kept in oral memory and written down after many centuries. It was when Brāhmī was used to represent the sounds of Sanskrit that the enduring features of Brāhmī seem to have been introduced. The linguistic design of Brāhmī has persisted through all the innovations in all its derivatives. What are the features of Brāhmī which have survived through historical evolution over centuries and characterize its derivatives used in present-day India? What is obvious is that the arrangement of the units is based entirely on ancient Indian phonetics, which is remarkably modern. Since the practice of Vedic recitation was a core cultural practice, phoneticians observed the physiology of sound articulation and classified the sounds of Sanskrit accordingly.

The arrangement of sounds according to phonetic classes was called *varnamala*. Phoneticians were aware of how different sounds were articulated in actual speech production and they formulated their knowledge in various treatises called *Pratishakhyas* and *Shikshas*. The *Pratishakhyas* were phonetic manuals for Vedic recitation, while the *Shikshas* were devoted to general phonetic processes. Each *Pratishakhya* is associated with a Veda and, in some cases, the specific recension. They discuss the phonetic and morphophonemic processes in the continuous and the segmented texts of the Veda in question. The *varnamala* was available long before the creation and use of Brāhmī. Yaska mentions the *varnamala* in *Nirukta* (a treatise on lexicology), which precedes the *Pratishakhyas* and Panini in chronology (Verma, 1971). Actually, Panini's *Aṣṭadhyāyī* opens with a set of *sutras* called *akṣarasamamnaya* (an ordered set of sounds). The *varnamala* is the inventory of the sounds of Sanskrit, arranged in terms of place (bilabial, dental, palatal, etc.) and manners of articulation (aspirated-unaspirated, voiced-voiceless). The formation of the *varnamala* suggests that the language scholars assumed that the mid-central vowel schwa was inherent in every consonant. Figures 3.1 and 3.2 show the Gujarati *varnamala* and Kannada *varnamala* respectively.

Children memorize the *varnamala* either at home or at school, regardless of what they are required to do by the local school boards. When I was in primary school the whole class recited the *varnamala* rhymically and loudly at the end of every school day. The arithmetic tables were also memorized and recited in the same fashion.

SCHWA (ə): MID-CENTRAL VOWEL

Perhaps the most obvious feature is the way the neutral vowel schwa is assumed to be inherently involved in all the consonants, unless indicated otherwise. The term "schwa" in Hebrew means the shortest vowel; hence, it is considered to be neutral. Some reading specialists who emphasize the central role of the "alphabetic code" in reading instruction applaud the designer(s) of Brāhmī. They argue that it is impossible to pronounce the consonants by themselves and it makes

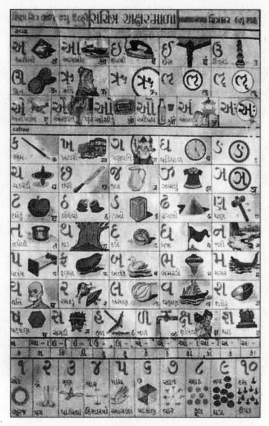

Figure 3.1
Gujarati *Varnamala*

sense to add schwas to consonants. The presence or absence of the schwa is marked differently in Indo-Aryan and Dravidian scripts. For example, in Gujarati and Devanagari, the presence of schwa is assumed, that is, not indicated; the absence of schwa in these scripts is indicated by a superscript diacritic called *halant* under the consonant at the end of words. *Halant* means "injured" and it is used to remove the inherent schwa associated with the consonant. The use of the *halant* to indicate the absence of the schwa is not common to all the Brāhmī scripts in India. On the other hand, some scripts indicate the presence of schwa. In the Telugu, Kannada, and Malayalam scripts of south (Dravidian) India, for example, it is the presence of the schwa

Figure 3.2
Kannada *Varnamala*

that is indicated. In general, a superscript check is placed over most consonants.

akṣarə AS AN ORTHOGRAPHIC UNIT

The concept of *akṣarə* in ancient Indic language science forms the basis of minimal written units in Brāhmī, and it initially stood for a spoken unit. In ancient Greece, similarly, the term *grammata* (letters) stood for both the spoken and written segments (Allen, 1981). In the Rgveda, the term *akṣarə* was used to refer to the vowel. Detailed descriptions of how to specify syllable structure in Sanskrit have been provided by the *Pratishakhya* scholars (Chakrabarti, 1996).

The *Pratishakhyas* were composed as phonetic manuals to provide guidance in articulation and accentuation, which were necessary in Vedic recitation and memorization (see Patel, 1996, for a brief account). The Rgveda *Pratishakhya* stipulates that a vowel, whether pure or combined with consonants or *anusvara* (nasalization), is an *akṣarə* (Mahulkar, 1981). The distinctions between short and long vowel as well as light and heavy syllables were also recognized and incorporated in the design of Brāhmī.

The ancient Hindu scholars were masters of metrical composition and word phonology. Following the available phonological scholarship, the creators of Brāhmī divided the syllable into two units, the consonant + vowel body and the following consonant. The first part consisting of the consonant + vowel in syllable structure was taken as an orthographic unit, *akṣarə*. The following consonant was allowed either an *akṣarə* status or was moved to the onset of the next consonant + vowel. Earlier, I had referred to the concept of *matra* as the primary measure of duration. The *matra* values of the *akṣarə* are as follows:

one *matra*: cv, ccv, cccv, v, c (a postvocalic, long consonant)
two *matras*: cvv, ccvv, cccvv, vv

In the name *Chaula* [chəula], the *akṣarə*s are [chəu] and [la]; the first *akṣarə* [chəu] is a diphthong, hence it contains two *matras*. And in the word *mala* [mālā], the vowel [ā] is long (aa) in the two *akṣarə*s [maa] and [laa], hence, both the *akṣarə*s carry two *matras*.

ANUSVARA IN *akṣarə* FORMATION

As a single unit, the *akṣarə* encodes v or vv with or without a preceding consonant or a consonant cluster. For *akṣarə* formation, vc and cvc syllables are decomposed into v and c and cv and c, respectively. The *anusvara*, the nasalization dot or a circle, is a sole exception to this elegant rule in most scripts. The *anusvara* as a nasal consonant occurs in the coda position. In most of the Brāhmī scripts, it is used to nasalize a vowel or as a nasal consonant homorganic with a following stop consonant. In the Devanagari and Gujarati scripts, the *anusvara* is represented as a dot placed over an *akṣarə*. In the Kannada script, the *anusvara* is an independent *akṣarə* represented by a circle; the *anusvara* əkʂərə stands in words like any other əkʂərə (Prakash et al., 1993). There are other Brāhmī scripts, which follow the same practice.

TOPOGRAPHIC ORGANIZATION OF *əkʂərə*s

The topography of the *əkʂərə*, that is, the visuospatial components and their organization forming orthographic units is as interesting as its linguistic design. In the early stages of the development of Brāhmī as a script, the vowels were added onto the consonants at the edges as markers. In the modern form of the different scripts derived from Brāhmī, the vowels are added on at the top, at the bottom, at the left, and at the right. To take illustrations from the modern forms of Brāhmī, the *əkʂərə*s for the consonant /k/ are formed as follows:

Devanagari Script

क	का	कि	की	के	को	कौ	कु	कू	कं	कः
kə	ka	ki	kii	ke	ko	kəu	ku	kuu	kəm	kəhə

Gujarati Script

ક	કા	કિ	કી	કે	કો	કૌ	કુ	કૂ	કં	કઃ
kə	ka	ki	kii	ke	ko	kəu	ku	kuu	kəm	kəhə

In topographic organization, the different scripts derived from Brāhmī fall into two main groups. In one group, dominated by the Indo-European linguistic branch, for example, Sanskrit, Hindi, and Marathi, which use the Devanagari script, the *əkʂərə*s are vertical in orientation. While in the other group, dominated by the Dravidian linguistic side, the topographic orientation is horizontal and circular, as in Tamil, Telugu, Kannada, and Malayalam. To appreciate this difference in topographic orientation, look at the letter shapes in the Gujarati *varnamala* and Kannada *varnamala* presented earlier.

What is characteristically important in the topographic design of Brāhmī *əkʂərə*s is the way vowels are placed around the consonants. The vowels and consonants are not placed sequentially as independent letter units in words, as it is done in Roman and other European scripts. In Brāhmī, *əkʂərə*s are spatial configurations which stand as independent units in a sequence.

Chapter Four

EMERGENCE OF READING IN LANGUAGE DEVELOPMENT

INTRODUCTION

Current research on reading acquisition treats the concept of phonological awareness as an isolated phenomenon without any link with language development. I will try to show that phonological awareness is picked up from cultural ecology as reading emerges in language development. This is particularly relevant in the case of mainstream Hindu children, for whom the Vedic oral tradition provides such a linguistic–cultural ecology, as they participate in most of the adult cultural–religious rituals. This idea is also implicit in the cumulative research record on the child's ability to segment utterances into phrases, words, syllables, and phonemes in relation to reading acquisition, in particular, and cognitive development, in general (Fox and Routh, 1975; Helfgott, 1976; Kirshenblatt-Gimblett, 1976; Rosner and Simon, 1971; Soderberg, 1971; Wolfenstein, 1954).

Language emerges and develops naturally in early childhood, given a normal genetic endowment and linguistic input in human inter-action. In the beginning, it is all crying, cooing, and babbling, followed by one and two word utterances. Grammatical morphemes and syntactic patterns join the ongoing process and somewhere in the pathway the process of the recognition of printed words emerges. During the course of this development, the child's language is in tune with environmental changes. As the child's language matures, the language used by the caretakers becomes increasingly complex. Interaction with the "mother" and the family is extended to the community and beyond. Within four or five years, depending upon the society, schooling influences the child and guides her towards the world of literate intelligence.

PRODUCTION AND PERCEPTION IN INFANCY

Speech production emerges in the form of the infant cry. Shortly after birth, perhaps in a month's time, the infant starts using the cry to express its needs. It manipulates the pitch or the fundamental frequency to create at least six different types of cry to express hunger, need for attention, discomfort, etc. The cry expressing comfort and pleasure is melodious, while the other types are high-pitched (see Lester and Zachariah-Boukydis, 1985, for accounts of research and references). The cry is a continuous prosodic unit marked by changes in the pitch pattern. The cry depends upon timing patterns for utterances as prosodic units, not segmental sounds or words.

What is called "motherese," that is, infant-directed speech, is remarkable for its prosodic characteristics, which make the boundaries of syntactic clauses so obvious. Research shows that infants respond to adult speech, which clearly indicates clause boundaries (Hirsch-Pasek et al., 1987). Trehub and Trainor (1993, p. 313) characterize infant speech perception as "extracting the pitch contours of melody." Cutler and Mehler (1993, p. 105) hypothesize that "It may be the case that the characteristic rhythm pattern of a language is sufficiently salient to assist the newborn child in segmenting the continuous speech stream into discrete units."

BABBLING, SYLLABLES, AND WORDS

The continuous timing pattern of the cry is broken when babbling emerges. Babbling consists of basic syllabic units carried over by prosodic melody. Initially, the syllabic and prosodic patterns are universal, but soon the infant begins to respond to the prosodic characteristics of motherese, that is, the infant-directed speech typically used by mothers while interacting with their infants. It is in this context that a baby becomes a member of a given speech community, that is, Assamese, Hindi, Kannada, etc., by the age of nine months or so. Within the melodic pattern of the utterance, the syllable appears as the first segmented linguistic unit in child language. This unit is an acoustic pattern which gives rise to the linguistic basis of the syllable.

Soon words are acquired which require production as well as storage mechanisms. Research indicates that the child's initial mental dictionary is like "a mental video library" (Griffith, 1986, p. 298). The child stores words and utterances in association with the seen or heard contexts or episodes. Obviously, this system of episodic storage cannot continue for long as the size of the child's mental dictionary keeps growing. As far as English-speaking Canadian children are concerned, Anglin (1993) estimates that first-graders know over 10,000 entries from Webster's unabridged dictionary; the figure doubles for each grade level. The pathway from infant cry to emergent literacy appears to be marked as shown in Model 4.1.

Model 4.1
Between Infant Cry and Emergence of Reading

Cry: Pitch patterns

Cooing: Infant-mother exchange through pitch patterns

Babbling: Syllables in pitch patterns

First 50 Words: Phonological frame

Basic Child Grammar: Syntactic patterns–functional morphemes–semantic relations

Spurt in Vocabulary Growth: From videos to words: mental dictionary being read to and verbal play

Written Input and Word Recognition: Emergent literacy: reorganization of the mental lexicon

CULTURAL ECOLOGY AND LINGUISTIC UNITS IN SPEECH

What is certain is that the language input available to the child carries clear markers for syllabic units and their melodic arrangements in all cultures. Children's literature contains phonological gibberish, which highlights syllabic divisions. Speech games like Pig Latin and Ubby Dubby are available in all languages and cultures (Kirshenblatt-Gimblett, 1976). The infant-mother interaction involves face-to-face communication while the mother is either taking care of the infant or enjoying the infant's company. This period of "primary subjectivity" overlaps the time when the infant begins cooing, an exchange of well-timed dyads between the mother and the infant (Trevarthen, 1977). Bates (1979, p. 12) suggests that "from the first few weeks of life mother and child are calibrated to one another in intricate patterns of turn taking and protolanguage."

As the infant grows into babyhood and childhood, the mother communicates and interacts with the child using regular social–linguistic routines which are about "here and now" objects, individuals, and contexts (Snow and Ferguson, 1977). The siblings and the street peers enter the interactive communication process, which introduces rhymes, speech games, moron jokes, and riddles (Wolfenstein, 1954). As the child matures in psycholinguistic development, the nature of the verbal play changes systematically (Kirshenblatt-Gimblett, 1976; Wolfenstein, 1954). As Sanches and Kirshenblatt-Gimblett (1976) point out, young children prefer purely phonologically motivated gibberish in speech play:

A B C D E F G,
H I J K L M N O P,
Q R S and T U V
Double-U and X Y Z.
Happy Happy we shall be
When we learn our A-B-C's.

Inty, ninty tibbety fif
Deema dima doma nig
Howchy powchy domi nowday
Hom tom tout
Olligo boligo boo
Out goes you.

Hickory, dickory, dock,
The mouse ran up the clock.
The clock struck one, the mouse ran down,
Hickory, dickory, dock.

In addition to speech games like Pig Latin and Ubby Dubby, there are jump-rope games, counting games, and clapping games played and enjoyed by children in different cultural–linguistic groups all over the world (Burling, 1966). All this speech play involves prosodic patterns, which depend upon well-marked syllable boundaries and timing. The linguistic units governing this child–child and child–adult verbal play are syntactic clauses and syllables. Obviously, what the child hears and how the child processes the speech signal involve segmentation into clause and syllable units.

akṣara IN HINDU CULTURAL ECOLOGY

In modern India, the metrical basis of Vedic composition pervades children's poetry, folk songs, wedding songs, and so on. This is a significant part of the cultural input that mainstream Hindu children receive. In India, children are allowed to attend family and community gatherings and are thereby exposed to religious and other ceremonies which involve recitation. The metrical composition and recitation of these different forms of input in cultural ecology available to children revolves around the *akṣara*. Children hear the *akṣara* clearly demarcated in this input; in the accentuation pattern, the *akṣara* is raised, lowered, or continued. Some ceremonies also have certain hand movements which correspond to the accentuation pattern. Children also memorize and recite poems and songs, which are composed along the same metrical principles. Consider the following illustrations:

Gayatri Mantra (Vedic Sanskrit)
ta tsa vi tu rva re nyam bha rgo de va sya di ma hi
dhi yo yo nah pra cho da ya t

Gujarati Grade One Poem
ja la ka ma la da la chhan di ja ne ba la
swa mi ha ma ro ja ga she
ja ga she ta ne ma ra she
ma ne ba la ha tya la ga she.

Gujarati Wedding Song
a kha nda ra he jo e
va ra ka nya nun jo dun

Gujarati Poem included in Gandhiji's Prayer
vai shna va ja na to tene re ka hi ye
je pi da pa ra i ja ne re

Gujarati Folk Song (Garba)
kha ma ma ra nan da ji na lal
mo ra li kya re va ga di

All these poems and songs are recited or sung melodiously, following metrical patterns which are derived directly from the ancient oral tradition. That is, the *akṣərə*s rise, fall, and get elongated according to the Vedic metrical rules. Children are always exposed to such a linguistic–cultural ecology.

Also relevant is the formulaic nature of much of the Vedic composition which helps the child's awareness of the *akṣərə* as a unit. The following example of what Bloomfield (1916) calls Rgvedic repetitions may not be infrequent in the *mantra*s, prayers, children's poems, wedding songs, folk dance songs, and so on:

eko vishvashya bhuvanashya raja
tena vishvashya bhuvanashya raja
somo vishvashya bhuvanashya raja
asya vishvashya bhuvanashya raja

Also drawing children's attention to the *akṣərə* are the speech games which they play with their peers. For example, the different speech games in Gujarati break up words into *akṣərə*s and manipulate their positions. In the first example in the following games, the words *mari*, *nishal*, and *bahadur* are segmented into *akṣərə*s and certain elements like "sm" are inserted after the first *akṣərə*.

Speech Games in Gujarati
mari = masmari = ma **sma** ri
nishal = nismishal = ni **smi** shal
bahadur = basmahadur = ba **sma** hadur
miran = mi*ngami*ran = mi **ngami** ran
nishal = ni*ggarmi*shal = ni **ggarmi** shal
sarun = *cha*sa*cha*run = **cha** sa **cha**run
nishal = *cha*ni*cha*sha*cha*l = **cha** ni **cha** sha **cha** l
khorakpani = *cha*kho*cha*ra*cha*ka*cha*pa*cha*ni
cha kho **cha** ra **cha** pa **cha** ni

In Malayalam, a Dravidian language, there is a secret code language called pa, in which pa is inserted before every *akṣərə* (Mohanan, 1986). For example,

kancan = pakapancan = **pa** ka **pa** ncan
indirɑ = payipandipara = **pa** yi **pa** pandi **pa** ra
susmita = **pa**su**pa**smi**pa**ta = **pa** su **pa** smi **pa** ta
moohanan = **pa**moo**pa**ha**pa**nan = **pa** moo **pa** ha **pa** nan

Chapter Five

COGNITIVE–LINGUISTIC–NEURAL PROCESSING IN READING

INTRODUCTION

As children acquire speech patterns from the input available to them, they are exposed to printed language, and they learn to read just as they learn to use speech. Most children who have no developmental difficulties involving the auditory and the visual processing systems, and have access to school, pass through the different phases in literacy acquisition with ease.

Reading is a language processing system: It involves neural–cognitive–linguistic subsystems related to script topography, orthographic structure, mental dictionary, grammatical system, general and domain-specific knowledge, relational–inferential processing, and so on. The visuospatial components and their organization (that is, script topography) encoding orthographic units represent the linguistic units underlying words. Words are connected to both meaning and grammar; these, in turn, are connected to domains of information and mechanisms of reasoning. These components need a representational system, which can facilitate long-term storage and speedy search and retrieval. In order to understand the products of reading, namely, comprehension and decoding, it is necessary to have a grasp of the subsystems and their network interconnections functioning in language processing. More particularly, the emergence and development of reading problems, in general, and dyslexia, in particular, can be better conceptualized and interpreted within such an integrated cognitive–linguistic–neural framework. This understanding also leads to the construction of theoretically productive tasks and stimuli for research studies.

EPISODIC–SEMANTIC SYSTEMS IN MEMORY

Daily social interactions with people who we know well involve, mainly, automatic speech (face-to-face or telephone conversations) or writing (language use in e-mail exchanges or postal correspondence with friends or family). They primarily require procedural memory, which is a set of habits or skills. When you meet a friend, you don't wait to decide how you are going to greet her. You just start and say whatever is specific to the context. You talk about the weather, vacations, weddings, and so on; you do not talk about Vedic mathematics or organo-metallic chemistry. In order to deal with such topics, you need attention, effort, and knowledge; these topics are discussed in specific professional contexts. Language functioning, including reading, in the daily life of mature literate language users involves procedural memory to a large extent. This type of memory based on skills and habits is different from what is called declarative knowledge, which consists of the episodic and semantic components (Tulving, 1985).

I remember my first day in elementary school: the principal (a lanky man with a cap, a long coat, and a yellow Hindu mark on his forehead), the teacher, my father's beaming face, a sack of crystal sugar, and the ceremony. Without any effort I can recall the way the priest chanted the invocation to Sarasvati, the goddess of learning, with attention to the articulation of every *akṣara*. So also can I recall the context in which I saw or heard the words like "viscid gloom" (James Joyce), "congenital synthesizer" (Edward O. Wilson), "pullutate" (Richard F. Gombrich), etc. This is episodic memory, which is formed on the basis of events, which occur just once in specific contexts.

When you try to involve your mental dictionary or some specialized domain of knowledge, for example, the grammatical system, the human genome, etc., you are using what is called semantic (generic) memory. This system deals with language and cognition. The linguistic system may include the domains of phonology (sound units and patterns), morphology (word composition), orthography (encoding of units and patterns in script topography with direct or indirect links to the dictionary), the lexicon, and syntax (categories and their relations in sentence organization). On the other side, the cognitive system may include subsystems dealing with perceptual mechanisms, inferential processing, and general–specialized knowledge. It must also include "prototypes," which may serve as a bridge between the cognitive and the linguistic sides. Prototypes are the best exemplars; for example, for North Americans, the prototypes for the categories of men's clothing, fruit, and four-footed animals, are shirt, apple, and dog, respectively.

Working Memory in Language Processing

Language use also needs what is called working memory for both production (speaking–writing) and comprehension (listening–reading). For comprehension, you need to have a limited passive system (a few seconds), which simply stores fragments of incoming information and feeds it in chunks to the central processing unit (Andrade, 2001; Baddeley, 1986). The central processing unit is connected to all the components of the episodic–semantic memory systems. As the incoming information enters the central processing unit via the passive articulatory rehearsal storage, all the relevant stored information is activated and retrieved. The incoming chunks are processed and integrated, which leads to comprehension, either complete or partial.

The language processing system needs a short-term working memory subsystem to operate. The components of the working memory system retrieve the relevant activated information from the long-term semantic memory storage files and link it with the heard or seen incoming input. The input in listening as well as in reading is received in chunks and processed with the help of the information from semantic memory. Model 5.1 provides a schematic view of working memory.

Model 5.1
Working Memory

	Comprehension	
Listening	Articulatory Rehearsal	Central Processing Unit
Reading	Visual Scratch Pad	
	Production	
Speaking	Articulatory Rehearsal	Central Processing Unit
Writing	Visual Scratch Pad	

LANGUAGE STRUCTURE AND PROCESSING

Before we consider the psycholinguistic processes involved in reading, let us look at what language structure and functioning entail. The faculty of language is a network of several structural layers with their counterparts related to grammatical and communicative networks and pathways. This applies to language in speech, writing, and signs. Model 5.2 shows what language structure and functioning contain.

Model 5.2
Language Structure and Functioning

Phoneme Mora ⟵ Syllable Morpheme	Orthographic Units
Word Sentence	Lexical Meaning Relational Meaning Syntactic Patterns Implicational and Inferential Meaning
Discourse	Discourse Types Genres Social–Cultural–Political Routines and Constraints

In writing, sound blocks are replaced with orthographic blocks, which may or may not have interdependent correspondences. As soon as you spot a written word, you are automatically connected to the mental dictionary. Even without paying attention and even if you have caught it only in your peripheral vision, you can access its lexical–relational meaning and grammatical category (e.g., noun, verb). There is a solid, cumulative record of robust research findings on lexical processing in English which shows that the meaning-level characteristics of words like concreteness, imageability, familiarity, and frequency have an effect in modulating word recognition processes (Balota, 1990; Chiarello, 1991). Experimenters have demonstrated that you can access the meaning of words even if they are masked, that is, when you do not have access to all the letters and their sequence; in other words, as a mature literate language user, you can bypass the process of decoding to reach meaning, that is, without transforming the written form into spoken form.

Whether words can be recognized directly without first transforming orthographic units into sound units is a relevant question, which has attracted many researchers. This is true in the case of research on both mature functioning in adults, and beginning stages in learning to read in children. Perfetti et al., (1988, p. 59) focus on the question of "whether phonetic activation occurs routinely as a part of lexical access." Their study suggests that a high degree of phonetic activation always occurs during lexical access, "never being wholly delayed until some 'moment of access' and never being omitted" (p. 68). Perfetti and Bell (1991, p. 484) make a strong claim about the time course of "phonemic activation" in word recognition: They claim 30 ms for real words and 35–45 ms for pseudowords. According to Perfetti and Zhang (1991), this is true even in the case of Chinese words written in logography, which primarily involves a semantic representation of morphemes, and secondarily, clues for pronunciation.

Psycholinguistic research on lexical processing without any reference to "phonetic activation" and its link to "decoding" suggests a set of findings, which together form the basis of Marslen-Wilson's (1989) "cohort" model. It focuses on the initial portion of the word which can be a morpheme or syllable or mora or phoneme, and the early recognition point occurs within 200 ms. The word-initial cohort involves the activation of all the words with similar spelling patterns; it is out of this group of words that the appropriate word is selected. The syntactic–semantic properties of this selected word are automatically activated and retrieved from semantic memory.

The process of word recognition in mature readers is extremely fast. Studies, which examine eye movements in reading, suggest that the observed time is 150–175 ms; however, the actual time taken to recognize words is only 50 ms (Rayner and Pollatsek, 1989). Equally important, the process of word retrieval carries a great deal of related information, which plays a crucial role in comprehension or misunderstanding. When you recognize verbs in reading sentences or paragraphs, you have also automatically retrieved information about their connections with nouns in relation to what, who, where, and so on. For example, the verb "like" implies a subject (who) and an object (what), while the verb "sleep" implies only a subject.

To understand sentences and paragraphs the reader needs to get into inferential processing. The sentence "My friend has managed to find her purse" logically entails that the friend's purse was lost. Implications may also be "nondemonstrative"; that is, they are interpreted intuitively based on your knowledge of the world around you. For example, when I say "At my age, we don't buy green bananas, as the saying goes," people can infer that I must be mature, that is, age-advanced. ("By the time the bananas are ready to eat, you might not be around.") Since I use terms like "mature" and "age-advanced" and avoid the "o" word ("old"), you can also draw an inference about my positive attitude to ageing as a natural process. My choice of words is guided by the prevailing social attitude toward mature age, which presupposes that "old age" implicates a feeble mind in a frail body. If you have come across Art Linkletter's book *Old Age is Not for Sissies*, you might think that I must be influenced by it.

In reading, as soon as you recognize words you are inside your linguistic–cognitive–neural system with all its components and processing mechanisms. As you progress in reading, your comprehension increases and you can then construct a model of it. This model can also help you to transform language from its written form into its speech form. The process underlying oral reading is generally known as "decoding," that is transforming orthography into speech, usually, using grapheme to phoneme correspondences. The products of reading (comprehension and decoding) depend upon the stage of learning in literacy development, especially in children. The phase during which children acquire the ability to decode orthography into phonology seems to be necessary in learning to read (Doehring, 1976).

Comprehension and Decoding in Children

In children's psycholinguistic development, comprehension precedes production. It seems to be the same in the case of reading. Only a handful of children (one in 100 in Scotland, the USA, and Canada) learn to read at home around the age four or so; these precocious readers can decode as well as comprehend what they read (Patel, 1977a; Patel and Patterson, 1982). The majority of children, including the brightest, begin to read when they join grade school. It is during this period in childhood, around age seven, that they begin to mature in neural–cognitive–linguistic development (Patel, 1977b).

The input from cultural ecology, especially in India where children are allowed to be with adults in family and community gatherings, provides information about interesting mythological characters and events. Children create knowledge domains in their semantic memory. For example, children hear so much about heroes and devils from the epics Ramayana and Mahabharata. The characters, Rama, Sita, Hanuman, Ravana, Krishna, Arjun, Bhim, Draupadi, for example, are vivid in their mental representation. When they are given reading materials which depict these characters and events, the children use this internal information to comprehend with minimal cues from decoding. For example, if a Gujarati child is asked to read a selection about the adventures of Hanuman or Bhim, the information that the child has picked up from the family and the community surely gets the young reader connected. The domain of knowledge related to the father of the Indian nation, that is, Mahatma Gandhi, in the episodic–semantic memory system facilitates reading comprehension in this case.

Again in India, the *akṣarǝs* are picked up from ecology as well as introduced in grade one, and children begin grappling with reading comprehension which brings them confidence. The complex *akṣarǝs* and words are not introduced until grade three. The phonologically transparent *akṣarǝs* in frequent, familiar words, simple syntactic patterns, and stories about familiar characters foster reading comprehension and nurture the process of reading acquisition. When I was in elementary grade school, all the stories and poems were presented in this mode. The poems were first acquired orally and the stories were heard at family or community functions. The poems and stories in current textbooks seem to be changing to suit the norms of political correctness. The children are still expected to memorize the poems, but the stories are fast moving away from traditional topics.

The question of the role and relevance of decoding is much more crucial in the case of children. You may recall our discussion on the importance of sound unit segmentation in the initial stage of learning to read. Golinkoff and Rosinski (1976) looked at the relationship between single-word decoding, single-word semantic processing, and text comprehension in third and fifth graders. This study suggests that "... decoding and semantic processing are separable processes and that, although less skilled comprehenders have difficulty decoding, this does not result in difficulties in accessing meaning." Golinkoff and Rosinski (p. 257) conclude that children who are less skilled in comprehension can "automatically pick up the meaning of printed words."

Barron and Baron (1977, p. 593) indicate that children can grasp the relationship between printed words and their meanings "very rapidly, perhaps with only two or three exposures." As for the role of orthographic structure in the development of visual word recognition, Barron's (1981, p. 129) analysis of research literature shows that

> sometime between the second and the fourth grade children seem
> to be able to use some of the gross characteristics of ortho-
> graphic structure, but it appears to be critically dependent on
> using three-letter items with CVC structures.

Furthermore, children develop the ability to attend to "several different units of processing (e.g., spelling patterns, syllables, some morphemes)" during grades two to four; this ability "coincides with the development of the use of orthographic structure" (pp. 137–38). Of crucial significance and relevance is Barron's suggestion that

> beginning readers may be somewhat more efficient at using
> visual than phonological information in word meaning access,
> whereas more mature readers may be more likely to use both
> visual and phonological information. (*ibid.*, p. 145.)

This is true in the case of Japanese children who learn to recognize the meaning-based kanji characters as well as the hiragana and katakana symbols, which are sound-based (morabaries). Steinberg et al., (1977) looked at the way three- and four-year-old nursery school children in Hiroshima processed kanji words (nouns, verbs, and adjectives) and individual hiragana symbols. Results clearly show that whether a word is written in kanji or kana is irrelevant for the Japanese readers beginning to read. What matters in the recognition of kanji and kana words is meaningfulness: Japanese children in nursery schools access the meaning of printed words with ease regardless of the variable of perceptual complexity. It seems that decoding and comprehension in reading acquisition go hand in hand in reality.

NEURAL PROCESSING IN READING

Reading is cognitive–linguistic processing, which is carried out by a complex neural organization. The information picked up by the retinal cells in the eyes passes through specialized channels and reaches specific regions in the brain. Oral reading and reading comprehension involve many networks of areas in the left and right hemispheres and their visual and auditory pathways passing through the various stations on the way to the different related cortical areas.

The cortical surface in the left and right hemispheres is divided into lobes and regions. The first anatomical division in the upper level of the cortical convoluted surface is between the frontal lobe and the parietal lobe; the dividing boundary is called the fissure of Rolando. In the lower part of the surface, the Sylvian fissure separates the frontal lobe and the temporal lobe. The frontal lobe is the seat for speech articulation, sentence production, working memory, and so on. The temporal lobe is located under the parietal lobe. Adjacent to the boundaries of the posterior parietal and temporal lobes at the back of the head is the occipital lobe, which first receives visual information from the subcortical pathways. Figure 5.1 explains the division of the cortical lobes.

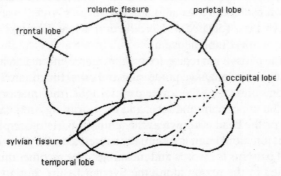

Figure 5.1
Cortical Lobes

The temporal lobe houses the primary auditory reception as well as the auditory association areas. The perisylvian region, which involves areas from the frontal, upper temporal, and the lower parietal lobes, is such a network. This region is associated with sound patterns for words and listening comprehension. The cortical perisylvian region with its subcortical substrates is responsible for both spoken language production and comprehension. Figure 5.2 shows the perisylvian region of the brain.

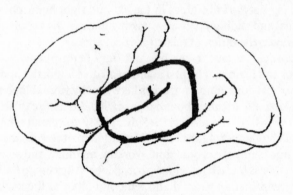

Figure 5.2
The Perisylvian Region

On the left side of the Sylvian fissure in the frontal lobe and on the right side of the Sylvian fissure in the temporal lobe are located what are known as "Broca's Area" and "Wernicke's Area," respectively. Broca's Area is associated with production, while Wernicke's Area is associated with comprehension.

After the perisylvian region follow the interconnected areas, which carry out written language processing and other functions. Similarly, the region connecting the lower parietal lobe (the inferior parietal lobule), the upper temporal lobe, and the adjoining occipital lobe at the back of the head is known as the temporo-parieto-occipital junction. This junctional unit is essentially associated with the processing of sound patterns for words and meanings, among other things.

Included in the region along the Sylvian fissure, horizontally as well as vertically, is the triangular area called the planum temporale, which is a part of the auditory processing cortical region. The planum temporale is located close to the primary auditory center called Heschl's gyrus. It receives auditory information transmitted through the medial geniculate nucleus in the thalamus and the inferior colliculus under it. The planum temporale contains a portion of Wernicke's Area as well as a part of Tpt. The Tpt belongs to the auditory association cortex. Research suggests that the asymmetry of the planum temporale favors the left hemisphere in right-handed people. The different cortical areas are known by the numbers assigned by Broadmann in his famous diagram shown in Figure 5.3.

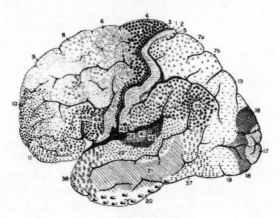

Figure 5.3
Broadmann's Areas

THE AUDITORY PROCESSING SYSTEM

In order to understand the process of learning to read and dyslexic performance, it is necessary to grasp the auditory pathway and its functions. There are two channels of information transmission associated with the processing of frequency and intensity in the acoustic speech stimulus. Frequency is transmitted by the nucleus magnocellularis, while intensity is carried by the nucleus angularis (Konishi, 1995). Auditory representation is tonotopic all through the different way stations (Rouiller, 1997). Model 5.3 explains the auditory processing system.

Model 5.3
The Auditory Processing System

Secondary Auditory Cortex (AII)	
Primary Auditory Cortex (AI)	
Thalamus:	Medial Geniculate Body (MGB)
	Lateral Part of the Posterior Nucleus of the Thalamus (PO)
Inferior Colliculus (IC):	Central Nucleus (ICC)
	Peripheral Nucleus (ICP)
	External Nucleus (ICX)
Choclear Nucleus (CN):	Anteroventral CN
	Posteroventral CN
	Dorsal CN
Superior Olivary Complex (SOC):	Lateral Superior Olivary Nucleus
	Medial Superior Olivary Nucleus
	Medial Nucleus of the Trapezoid Body
Lateral Lemniscus	
Cochlea:	Auditory Neurons Type I and Type II
Auditory Nerve:	Spiral Ganglion Cells

A note on the ipsilateral and contralateral pathways in the auditory system is warranted. The ascending central auditory system begins with the termination of the eighth nerve onto the secondary sensory neurons of the cochlear nuclear complex. The cochlear nuclei give rise to three pathways known as the acoustic striae. The striae traverse the brain stem sending axons to the superior olivary complex, the nuclei of the lateral lemniscus, and the inferior colliculus. Neurons of the superior olivary complex send their axons to the nuclei of the lateral lemniscus and to the inferior colliculus. The lateral lemniscus projects mainly to the inferior colliculus. Then, the inferior colliculus gives rise to the fibers, which go to the medial geniculate body in the thalamus, which, in turn, sends fibers to the auditory cortex. As Hutson (1997, p. 385) emphasizes,

> projections from the inferior colliculus through the auditory cortex remain, for all practical purposes, on the same or homo-lateral side of the brain: Therefore, above the level of the inferior colliculus there is no need to distinguish a substantial ipsilateral versus contralateral pathway.

Hutson (*ibid.*, p. 434) points out that "the acoustic chiasm is a process and not a structure." Various structures between the trapezoid body and the lateral lemniscus are responsible for the process of acoustic chiasm. This process transmits information specific to sound localization for which the different inputs from the two ears is necessary. The ipsilateral and the contralateral pathways are necessary for accurate sound localization in space. The ipsilateral pathways are biased toward low to mid-range frequencies. The ipsilateral projections arise from nuclei which tonotopically prefer low frequency acoustic stimuli. Within the cochlea, there is an orderly progression of sensitivity from low to high frequencies. This is the same for each subcortical auditory nuclei and the primary auditory cortex.

What is interesting is the influence of acoustic stimuli on the discharge rate of units located in the deep layers of the superior colliculus, which is a part of the visual system. These units are supposed to be sensitive to the cues for sound localization. Hence, the superior colliculus is considered to be the location of some form of auditory space representation in mammals (Rouiller, 1997). Between the auditory areas in the thalamus and the auditory cortex, there are three routes, which are tonotopic, non-tonotopic (diffuse), and multimodal. The superior olivary complex is the lowest level of the auditory pathway where a massive convergence of the information coming from both ears takes place. Perhaps a deeper understanding of the way the auditory and visual pathways interact and influence each other will lead to a comprehensive account of the time course of reading acquisition and the bottlenecks in dyslexic performance in learning to read.

THE VISUAL PROCESSING SYSTEM AND READING

For reading, you need the retinal ganglion cells, some specific subcortical structures, the occipital lobe, and then, the adjacent posterior lower temporal and parietal areas, which occupy more than half of the brain. At the back of the head in the occipital lobe is located the primary visual center, known as the striate cortex. The junctional regions bordering the striate cortex (the primary visual area) in the occipital, the parietal, and the temporal lobes are called "extrastriate" or prestriate areas. These visual areas are labeled V1, V2, V3, V4, and V5, which correspond to specific Broadmann's Areas (Buser and Imbert, 1992, pp. 392–97).

The information arriving at the striate cortex, which processes visual features, is passed on to the bordering extrastriate areas in the occipital, posterior parietal, and the inferior posterior temporal lobes. The term "oil refinery" is used to refer to the extensive interconnexions within the visual processing areas outside the primary visual center in the occipital lobe (Weiskrantz, 1997).

Recent research identifies the extrastriate region as a critically important locus in word recognition and is referred to as " prestriate visual word form system" (Carr and Posner, 1995; Petersen et al., 1990). This prestriate visual word form system responds to written words and orthographically regular pseudowords, but not to random strings of letters. It is active only during reading and produces no response to spoken words or pseudowords.

Posner and McCandliss (1999) suggest that the brain circuitry for the visual word form system in the left prestriate area can be demonstrated in 10-year-olds. While the visual word form system in adults codes an abstract orthographic form, the developing system at and before the age of 10 years "codes specific visual words" (*ibid.*, p. 330). These early words, coded visually by the prestriate word form system, involve mainly high frequency and familiar words. Associated with the transmission of high frequency information and the recognition of familiar/frequent words are the parvocellular pathway and the left hemisphere, respectively. You will read about this a bit later.

Under the cortical areas lie the various nuclei of the limbic system, which includes the hippocampus and the related structures that are associated with episodic memory. Located under the limbic structures are the different nuclei of the basal ganglia, which are involved in voluntary movement processes, for example, speech articulation, writing, and signing. The junctional station known as the thalamus is under the basal ganglia. The thalamic nuclei, the lateral geniculate nucleus (LGN), and the medial geniculate nucleus (MGN) transmit visual and auditory information, respectively. The third thalamic structure, the pulvinar, is also involved in reading, specifically in saccadic eye movements. The saccadic eye movements fixate at appropriate points and jump from word to word to pick up information for word recognition. The brain stem, which connects the bottom structures to the thalamus, includes the superior and the inferior colliculi, which transmit the visual and the auditory information, respectively. The cerebellum, which deals with specific movements and skill learning in conjunction with the rest of the brain, is located at the bottom. Model 5.4 shows the horizontal and vertical organization of the brain.

How does the information picked up by the retinal ganglion cells reach the different cortical areas? Model 5.5 explains the retinal-cortical pathway.

The ganglion cells are the output neurons of the retina. There are two major visual pathways one of which is phylogenetically older.

Model 5.4
The Horizontal–Vertical Organization of the Brain

Cortex: Frontal, Temporal, Parietal, and Occipital Lobes
Limbic System: Hippocampus, Amygdala, ...
Basal Ganglia: Globus Pallidus, Putamen, ...
Thalamus: Lateral Geniculate Nucleus, Medial Geniculate Nucleus,
Pulvinar
Superior Colliculus, Inferior Colliculus
Pons: Locus Ceruleus
Cerebellum

Model 5.5
From the Retina to the Cortex

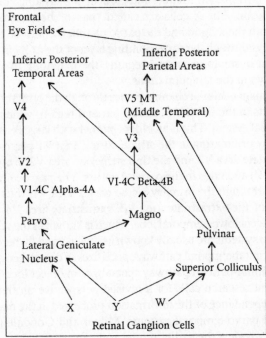

The major subcortical pathway contains direct projections from the retina to the superior colliculus. The axons of the retinal ganglion cells connect primarily with the superficial layers of the superior colliculus. The major cortical pathway runs from the retina to the lateral geniculate nucleus in the thalamus to the primary visual center known as the striate cortex, area V1. The retinal-cortical pathway consists of "two parallel and quasi-independent streams of processing: parvocellular and magnocellular" (Dannemiller, 2001. p. 226).

There are at least two types of retinal ganglion cells, X and Y. The X cells sustain responses for as long as the stimulus is present in the receptive field. The relatively small receptive fields in the X cells are sensitive to high spatial frequencies and their axons conduct slowly. In contrast, the Y cells respond transiently to visual stimuli and have relatively large receptive fields which are sensitive to low spatial frequencies; their axons conduct rapidly. Associated with the X and Y cells are the magnocellular and the parvocellular transmission channels. The Y cells magnocellular is a fast channel, which picks up transient low frequency information. These cells are called "magno" type cells because they are large in size. In contrast, the X cells parvocellular is a slow transmission channel and picks up the sustained high frequency information. The X cells are called "parvo" because of their small size. Both the magno and the parvo channels continue their separate pathways through the corresponding layer of the LGN in the thalamus and end in separate cortical regions, the magno in the parietal, and the parvo in the temporal areas.

The magnocellular channel passes through the primary visual cortex and ends in the inferior posterior parietal region, which is known as the dorsal system. This is an older channel with large cells. The magno pathway originating in the striate cortex area V1 passes through the extrastriate area V3 and the thin stripes of area V2 to area MT (mid-temporal) and ends in the parietal cortex. The parvocellular pathway crosses through the primary visual cortex area V1, the thin and pale stripes of the extrastriate area V2, extrastriate area V4, and reaches the adjacent lower temporal lobe, which is known as the ventral system. The two systems are usually known as "what" and "where" pathways: The occipital-temporal pathway specializes in object recognition, while the occipital-parietal pathway specializes in object location.

Recent research calls for a revised perspective on the question of the independence of the information processed in the magno-parietal and the parvo-temporal systems. Milner and Goodale (1995, p. 39) critically review the earlier model and suggest that,

Despite early suggestions of a continued anatomical segregation between the magno and parvo inputs both within the primary visual cortex and beyond, there is now considerable evidence that the two classes of input are heavily intermingled. The dorsal stream of projections from the striate cortex, through to the posterior parietal region, although largely magno in origin, also contains a significant, if small parvo input. The ventral stream of projections is even more mixed, with probably as many inputs from the magno as the parvo system.

This point regarding the interconnections between the magno and the parvo channels is particularly crucial in the context of what happens in dyslexic performance. The current interpretations in the dyslexia literature assume that the magno and the parvo channels are modular.

It must be noted that there are at least nine connecting links between the retina and the different processing areas in the brain. As pointed out previously, one of them transmits information from the retinal ganglion cells directly to the prestriate areas via the superior colliculus in the brain stem and the pulvinar in the thalamus. This stream ends in the frontal eye fields, a region situated in the anterior part of the frontal lobes (Weiskrantz, 1997). This information stream is supposed to guide eye movements.

The eye movements in reading fixate on specific points in words. The processes and mechanisms responsible for fixations in eye movements must be involved in the language processing subsystems, which process meaning and syntactic categories in reading. Hence, the retinal–superior colliculus–pulvinar–extrastriate pathway must be as important as the magnocellular–parvocellular pathways in reading. This point is usually ignored when the question of abnormal eye movements in some dyslexic children is discussed.

MAGNO–PARVO CHANNELS AND WORD PROCESSING

Now let us see the connection between the magnocellular–parvocellular channels and visual information processing for words in reading. The transient and sustained information transmission channels identified in psychophysics are the same as the magnocellular and parvocellular pathways identified in neurobiology. The functional distinction is crucial to understanding how reading takes place. Recall that the magnocellular-transient channel picks up information coded in low spatial frequencies, while the parvocellular-sustained channel picks up the information coded in high frequencies. The magno-transient passage is fast in information transmission, while the parvo-sustained channel is sluggish.

The magno-transient passage transmits word-specific features and a specific type of information from script topography; this is transmitted to the visual processing parietal areas in the right hemisphere. Recall that the right hemisphere processes word-specific features sequentially to recognize infrequent, long, and strange words. The slow parvo-sustained channel recognizes orthographic lexical forms of frequent short words in conjunction with the visual areas in the lower temporal lobe in the left hemisphere.

Breitmeyer and Lovegrove, among others, have developed a spatial-frequency analysis model of spatio-temporal processing within the fast preattentive stages of visual analysis, which relates to reading and dyslexia (Breitmeyer, 1989; Lovegrove et al., 1986; Slaghui et al., 1993). See Model 5.6.

Model 5.6
Transient (Magno) and Sustained (Parvo) Channels

Transient-Dorsal *Magnocellular*	*Sustained-Ventral* *Parvocellular*
• *Slow response*	• *Fast response*
• *Quick global processing*	• *Sequential processing*
• *Low spatial frequencies*	• *High spatial frequencies*
• *Operates preattentively and guides the sustained channel to focus on salient areas for pattern identification*	

Words are encoded in script topography, which is organized in terms of categorial and coordinate relations (Kosslyn, 1987). Roman letters, for example, are made up of certain basic categories; the shapes of the letters **b**, **d**, and **p** have the categories **c** and **l** in common, that is, the categorial shapes **c** and **l** are put together differently. Brāhmī *akṣara*s are also made up of common visual categorial shapes. These basic shapes are called categorial relations. The Roman letters and Brāhmī *akṣara*s are sequenced linearly to form words. The linear sequential positioning of letters or *akṣara*s is characterized in terms of coordinate relations. Research suggests that the left hemisphere processes categorial relations, while the right hemisphere deals with the coordinate relations. The abstract categorial system in the left hemisphere processes the lexical orthographic form of short frequent words (e.g., dog, beer, pizza, etc.), while the form-specific coordinate system in the right hemisphere processes the word-specific forms in infrequent and long words such as exculpatory, dissentual, consilience (Marsolek et al., 1992).

Left Hemisphere	*Right Hemisphere*
• Parvo-sustained processing	• Magno-transient processing
• Categorial relations	• Coordinate relations
• Abstract form	• Form-specific
• Orthographic-lexical	

No matter what form a script takes, it consists of categorial and co-ordinate relations, which represent the lexical-orthographic units. The Chinese and Japanese scripts are always taught in terms of the different strokes and the ways in which they are positioned.

When actually reading sentences in isolation, paragraphs or connected discourse, your eyes scan all the information in the topographic design of the letters or akṣarəs or logographs. This involves both the left and the right hemispheres, each picking up different types of information and words. As pointed out earlier, the left hemisphere recognizes, primarily, short, frequent, and familiar words (bread, butter, coffee) fast, while the right hemisphere scans the long, infrequent, and strange-looking words (viscid, sedulous, and diaphanous). As Chiarello (1991) suggests, words are encoded and examined as whole units in the right visual field or left hemisphere, but as serial letter strings in the left visual field or right hemisphere. In this context, there is also an important difference between the two hemispheres in word recognition processes. It is only in the left hemisphere that top-down feedback from lexical to orthographic units is available. Chiarello suggests that the lexical processes in the left hemisphere are important for two specific reasons: (*a*) selection of the most relevant sense in a given context from the group of activated meanings; (*b*) inhibition of irrelevant meanings. Semantically related words are activated automatically as a product of the recognition process.

The neurocognitive processing for reading involves several levels and mechanisms, which transform script topography into lexical orthography and leads to comprehension or oral output. The retinal ganglion cells provide different inputs to the magnocellular and parvocellular channels, which pass through the thalamus and the primary visual cortex. The output from the primary visual or striate cortex moves to the extrastriate areas where the visual features are transformed into orthographic word form. Then begins the processing for meaning and, if necessary, phonological form. Word recognition activates lexical meaning, semantic relations, and syntactic categorial information. That is, some basic syntactic information is activated along with lexical and relational meaning during word recognition when syntactic parsing operates in sentence and paragraph processing is still an open question (Clifton et al., 1994). In discourse reading, it is possible that lexical and syntactic processing levels are intermingled. What dominates discourse processing in reading is the need for inferential processing, which depends upon contexts and schemas (Kintsch, 1988).

Chapter Six

akṣaras AND CURRENT READING ACQUISITION RESEARCH

INTRODUCTION

The concept of phonological awareness is pivotal in the current models of reading acquisition in North America and Western Europe (Brady and Shankweiler, 1990; Goswami and Bryant, 1990; Gough et al., 1992). The focus so far has been on methodological correctness and quantitative data at the cost of conceptual clarity and adequacy. The perspective from subsyllabic scripts and the culture of oral learning raises important and consequential questions. Also relevant is the acoustic basis of segmental sounds and the way they are processed in the subcortical nuclei and the primary auditory cortex. The way it is conceptualized for experimental research and the nature of the linguistic unit associated with phonological awareness in the context of Brāhmī scripts calls for attention and reconsideration.

The akṣara encodes v, vv, cv, ccv, cccv, cvv, ccvv, cccvv, and c (only postvocalic long consonants) as visuospatial configurations. In Hindu India, the akṣara as a spoken unit is rooted in speech production and perception. A child's auditory perceptual system in routine Indian life is exposed to the akṣara as a spoken unit at different stages—when the child is a fetus, an infant, and as a child before and during the process of reading acquisition. The child walks into the pedagogic setting in school where the *akṣara* is encountered as a written unit. The *varnamala*, the phonetic inventory with the visual shape of each consonant and vowel of the language concerned, is introduced and recited regularly.

Most of the models of reading acquisition based mainly on the studies of children learning to read using the Roman script emphasize the role of segmental awareness associated with the alphabetic principle. The *akṣara* does not function in terms of the phonemic or alphabetic principle. The phonological–topographic organization of the *akṣara* as an orthographic unit gives rise to several issues which must be addressed in any attempt to model reading acquisition processes.

The research literature on reading acquisition is dominated by several strands, each with a well-defined program of research: (*a*) segmental awareness guided by phonemic theory and the alphabetic principle; (*b*) the role of auditory processing with reference to knowledge of rhymes; (*c*) phases in word recognition—from sight identification to the alphabetic principle; (*d*) models of syllabic division and segmental unit awareness; and, (*e*) analogy-based processes in word recognition learning.

Current Models of Reading Acquisition

The different models of reading acquisition in North America and Western Europe are based mainly on experimental logic and data involving the languages which use scripts based on the alphabetic principle. Guided by the logic of the alphabetic principle and phonemic theory, some researchers argue that children learning to read must learn to segment words into syllables and phonemes. The experimental studies motivated by this line of reasoning focused on the child's processing of the acoustic speech code and showed that children took some time to develop awareness about sound segments in words, especially phonemes (Liberman et al., 1974). The distinction between the concrete acoustic–articulatory level of phonetic segments and the abstract phonological level is usually not clarified. Hence, researchers use terms like phonological or phonemic awareness. The term "phonemic awareness" is dominant and it has generated some controversy.

The issue of the nature of the role of "phonemic awareness" in reading acquisition has given rise to the question: Is phonemic awareness a prerequisite or a consequence in learning to read? Later research has suggested an interactive link between phonological awareness and learning to read. The introduction of phonological theory into this research enterprise led to the perspective of the developmental course of segmental sound unit awareness.

The study by Liberman et al., (1974) showed that the syllable precedes the phoneme in phonological awareness: Syllabic awareness appears to be present by at least four years of age. Onset-rime awareness has been observed at age four and may emerge as early as ages two or three via experience with nursery rhymes (Bradley and Bryant, 1983; Maclean et al., 1987). Bowey and Francis (1991, p. 100) suggest that prereaders are sensitive to "subsyllabic composition of onsets and rimes," but not to phonemes, and sensitivity to onset and rime is "... a natural developmental phenomenon facilitating comprehension of reading instruction, which in turns, fosters phonemic sensitivity."

The research paradigm pioneered by Isabelle Liberman and Donald Shankweiler focused on speech segmentation tasks in children. The team led by Peter Bryant shifted attention from the acoustic speech code to children's auditory processing ability, clearly a step in the right direction; it helped them to raise crucially important research questions. For this, they pursued the ability to recognize nursery rhymes in association with the process of learning to read. They selected children who were one to three years behind their peers in reading acquisition and compared them with younger children of normal reading ability; the two groups were matched on IQ and reading level.

Bryant developed an "oddity task" which required identifying the "odd word out" from a set of four one-syllable words, three of which matched in initial consonant (sun, see, sock versus rag), and vowel (red, bed, versus no). Overall, 92 percent of the poor reading children made at least one error, 85 percent making more than one. Only 53 percent of the normally reading younger children made any errors at all, and only 27 percent made more than one. This difference was found even though the poor reading children were an average of three years older than the normally reading children. Bradley and Bryant's (1983) follow-up, a large-scale study, involved a longitudinal design and a training component: The children who received sound categorization training achieved significantly higher reading and spelling scores, with a greater advantage for those children who were trained in sound-letter relationships as well. Later, Maclean et al., (1987), Bryant et al., (1989), and Bryant et al., (1990) pursued the relationship between rhyming ability, phonological segmental awareness, and progress in learning to read. Results indicated "a highly specific relationship between a child's knowledge of nursery rhymes and his or her ability to detect rhyme" (Maclean et al., 1987, p. 271). The data also showed a relationship between rhyme detection at age three and early signs of reading 15 months later, regardless of general intelligence and family background.

The model of reading acquisition developed by Linnea C. Ehri based on her research looks at the different phases involved in word recognition. Ehri shows how the capacity for written word recognition in reading begins as a sight word learning process and develops into a "full alphabetic phase" in English:

> ... sight word learning begins as a nonalphabetic process involving memory for connections between selected visual cues and words. However, once learners acquire some knowledge about the alphabetic writing system, sight word learning changes into an alphabetic process involving connections between letters in written words and sounds in their pronunciations (Ehri, 1998, p. 17).

Ehri cites Reitsma's (1983) Dutch study which shows that first graders can retain sight words in memory after reading the words as few as four times. Ehri and Wilce (1983b) indicate that beginners recognize words by sight as whole units with no pauses between sounds within one second of seeing them. Sight word learning in Ehri's model is not based on rote learning and memory, as it is understood in the dual route view. According to the dual route theory, both irregularly and regularly spelled sight words are acquired through rote memory. Ehri's conceptualization and research on the acquisition of sight words during the initial phase emphasize that regularly as well as irregularly spelled words known to children by sight are recoded rather than read by sight. In Ehri's perspective, the alphabetic system of representation underlying English spelling is not dominated by irregularities and beginners need to learn how the alphabetic system works in order to succeed in learning to read. Ehri argues that the dual route theory cannot explain development in reading acquisition because it "... conceptualizes sight word reading as a separate, visually based route that neither involves nor requires phonological recoding ..." (1992, p. 112).

MODELS OF SYLLABLE STRUCTURE
AND READING ACQUISITION

A sizeable and influential body of research pioneered by Rebecca Treiman was motivated by the internal structure of the syllable as a phonological unit, as it was conceptualized in the linguistic theory dominant at the time. Based on her research on children's word games and other related verbal processes, Treiman suggested that the linguistic division of the syllable into onset and rime was natural, that is, it played a significant role in language processing: Children find it easy to segment syllables at the onset-rime boundary. Analysis of individual differences in their data led Treiman et al., (1990) to conclude that the "nature of orthographic units" is an issue "which any model of reading or of reading development must address" (p. 566).

In this context, Treiman et al., observed that it was the vc unit (nucleus + coda) rather than the cv unit (onset + nucleus) that was associated with the children's scores on the correct oral reading of nonsense words in English. Their logic that "... VC units correspond to a natural phonological constituent of the spoken syllable" (*ibid.*, p. 560) was fostered by Kiparsky's (1979, p. 436) hypothesis, which suggests that the association between the nucleus and the coda is a natural bond and is "closer compared to nucleus and onset." The rime was also an important concept earlier in structural linguistics for Kenneth Pike and Charles Hockett.

When 29 first graders from a public school serving a middle-class American English-speaking population around Detroit were asked to read nonwords with cv and vc units, they were superior in their performance vis-à-vis the vc sequences. The frequency of cv did not make a positive contribution in any of the analyses once the other variables were statistically controlled. On the other hand, as the frequency of the nonwords' vc increased, so did the children's correct pronunciation of the nonwords. The superiority of the vc units in recognition continued to be important at higher stages of reading acquisition.

The substance in the bridge between the onset-rime syllable theory and the data showing the superiority of the rime (vc) unit in reading acquisition developed by Rebecca Treiman is disputed in the model developed by Goswami (1998). Goswami moved the focus away from phonological rimes to orthographic rimes. You may recall that the phonological syllable is divided into onset and rime (nucleus + coda) where the onset and the coda consist of only consonants and the nucleus consists of a vowel, short or long. The orthographic rime is a spelling unit that corresponds to the spoken rime. Goswami's research suggests that very young readers typically use the analogical process based on orthographic rimes. This finding has been replicated in several studies (for example, Bowey and Hansen, 1994). Goswami argues that the functional importance of orthographic rimes in learning to read English written in the Roman alphabetic script can be accounted for in terms of the statistical properties of the English spelling system: The English orthography is highly regular at the level of the rime (vc). Treiman et al., (1995) suggest that rimes (vc units) in English have consistent pronunciation. Also notable in Treiman et al.'s analysis is the result that cv units are pronounced consistently only in 52 percent of the cvc words, even though the initial consonants in cv are predictable. Goswami cites Stanback (1992) who analyzed the different vc unit patterns in 43,041 syllables in the 17,602 words in Carroll et al.'s (1971) word frequency norms for children. Stanback found that the entire corpus could be described by only 824 vc units.

If the superiority of the vc unit in learning to read English can be attributed to the statistical properties of English orthography, it is interesting to see what happens in other languages which also use alphabetic scripts. Research conducted by Goswami in collaboration with her counterparts in French, Spanish, and Greek indicates that the superiority of the vc unit is specific to English orthography. Goswami et al., (1999) and Goswami et al., (1997) show that the effect of rime familiarity, that is, the vc unit, varies in English, French, Greek, and Spanish: In French and Spanish, which use the Roman alphabetic script, the rime effect was smaller compared to English, while there was no effect at all in Greek which uses a different alphabetic script.

The phonological design of the akṣara in Brāhmī scripts does not recognize the rime as a natural unit. It is based on a different model of syllable design, which puts the onset and the nucleus together as a unit, that is, the body, and the postvocalic consonant or consonant cluster is separated from this unit.

The principle of syllabic division underlying *akṣərə* formation can be accounted for in terms of syllable quantity and the *matra* as its primary measure. The *akṣərə* can either be one *matra* or two *matras*. A single *matra akṣərə* can be v with or without a consonant or a consonant cluster preceding it, that is, v, cv, ccv, cccv; a double *matra akṣərə* can be vv (long vowel or diphthong) with or without a consonant or a consonant cluster preceding them, that is vv, cvv, ccvv, cccvv. A single *matra akṣərə* can also be c, that is, a consonant by itself, but it cannot be just any consonant in a syllable structure; it has to be in the coda position where it can have a whole *matra* value: The consonant after the vowel either becomes an *akṣərə* or merges with the following consonant before the next vowel. At the end of word, the half-*matra* value of the consonant *akṣərə* is indicated with a diacritic under it. If the diacritic is absent, the reader is guided by the representation of the spoken word in her mental dictionary.

Perhaps the most obvious visuospatial characteristic of the *akṣərə* is that it stands as a whole unit in written words, which is a reflection of its phonological organization. Analytically, the phonemes in most of the *akṣərəs* can be identified. In visual perception, the reader picks up *akṣərəs* as units in a sequence. The *akṣərəs* are sequenced to form words without any spaces between them; they are "segmentation units" as are the moraic orthographic units in Japanese. For children at the beginning stage in reading acquisition, there is no struggle to segment words into individual orthographic units; they are given to them in segmented arrays. In topographic design, the *akṣərə* stands as a visual–spatial unit.

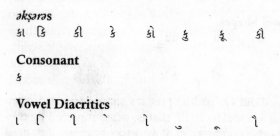

akṣərəs

Consonant

Vowel Diacritics

Yes, you can pull apart the vowels from the consonants; in most cases, you can identify the consonants and the vowels in *akṣarə*s. There are just a few exceptions with a unitary configuration. For example,

    ज्ञ   gn
    त्र   tr
    क्ष   ksh

This visuospatial configuration implies that there must be two forms of the vowel signs. For the *akṣarə* which stands for **v** alone, there are distinct shapes. For the other *akṣarə*s, the vowel signs, there are secondary shapes. These secondary shapes are such that they can be placed or joined with the consonants at the top, at the bottom, to the left, and to the right. That is, the onset consonants and the nucleus are organized hierarchically, not in a linear sequence as it is done in the alphabetic scripts, Roman or Cyrillic. In the alphabetic scripts, the letters are sequenced from left to right; you have to segment the sequence into linguistic units, which may be phonemes, syllables, or morphemes. In the case of the *akṣarə*, you have a given phonological unit. You can have a clear picture of the difference between the two shape types when you view the following illustration from Gujarati:

Primary Vowel Shapes

ə	I	ii	u	uu
અ	ઈ	ઈ	ઉ	ઊ
અડે	ઈડકી	ઈદ	ઉદર	ઊંચ

Note that the first vowel [ə] is an exception. The vowel [ɑ] does not have an independent form; it is formed by using the primary [ə] with its secondary shape, as in આ.

Secondary Vowel Shapes

a	i	ii	u	uu
ા	િ	ી	ુ	ૂ
આગ	દિન	દીન	દુધ	દૂખ

As has been pointed out earlier, the primary shapes are used when the *akṣarə* stands for a vowel by itself, that is, without preceding consonants. There are other complexities at work too, however, they need not detain us from our purpose.

Written words are sequences of *akṣarə*s. The *akṣarə* as an orthographic unit consists of a syllabic quantity unit—*matra*. The short vowel is a basic unit, which allows the long vowel or the diphthong two *matra*s. Depending upon the length, a consonant after the nucleus, that is, the vowel in syllabic organization, can be a full *matra*. When it does not have the quantity for a whole *matra*, it is integrated with the next onset, except at the end of words. In phonological terms, the process of *akṣarə* formation in lexical representation involves resyllabification. Note that the composition of each *akṣarə* remains the same in words; what changes is the structure of the syllables in words. *akṣarə*s do not respect morpheme boundaries. Suniti Kumar Chatterji points out (cited in Mahulkar, 1981, p. 66) that the word *dharma* contains two morphemes and two morae, which are not the same. He was bothered that morphological unity was not respected:

word	*dharma* "code of conduct"
*akṣarə*s	dha rma
morphemes	dhar ma

The phonological encoding of *akṣarə*s without any morphemic control is clearly illustrated in the following examples:

word	*karma* "action"
*akṣarə*s	ka rma cv cvc
morphemes	kar ma

word	*krama* "sequence"
*akṣarə*s	kra ma ccv cv
morphemes	kram

The words *karma* and *krama* are written as follows: Following the rules of *akṣarə* formation, the [r] is placed differently. This has a basis in the Pratishakhya scholarship:

ş·{	*karma*	kə rmə cv ccv
ş·ч	*krama*	krə mə ccv cv

Can the concept of *akṣara* have any significance in the processing system? Levelt and Wheeldon (1995) suggest that the language processing system for production includes a component which involves a "mental syllabary" for the native speakers of Dutch, which uses the Roman alphabetic script. For the speakers of the Indo-Aryan and Dravidian languages, which use Brāhmī scripts, it is a simple case. They are accustomed to *akṣaras* in their languages, hence, it is not unnatural to postulate a mental *akṣaramala* along the line of the *varnamala*. It is difficult to imagine another way of maintaining the metrical basis of language production without any conscious effort. Hence, for the native users of Brāhmī scripts, the language system for encoding (production) as well as decoding (recognition) presumably depends upon the mental *akṣaramala*.

Ignatius Mattingly, who appears to have created the notion of phonemic awareness, points out the fallacy in the way it has been conceptualized (mainly by his close associates) in experimental research. According to Mattingly (1978, p. 732), "... if a child counts syllables accurately, it is because he or she has access, not to unencoded acoustic information, but to representations of phonological syllables in a mental lexicon." The ability for sound segmentation may be related, not so much to reading by itself, but to the development of the mental dictionary. As Walley (1993, p. 287) argues, " the phonemic segment emerges first as an implicit, perceptual unit by virtue of vocabulary growth and only later as a more accessible, cognitive unit that can be consciously deployed in reading."

Phonological Awareness and Auditory Sound Processing

In considering decoding, that is, transforming spelling into segmental sounds, the question of the acoustic nature of the different segmental sounds cannot be ignored. Hirsh (1959) showed experimentally that auditory temporal resolution, that is, the perception of two sounds as distinct, and auditory discrimination, that is, the ability to perceive two different sounds as different, are basic in auditory sound processing. Paula Tallal's extensive program of research on language-impaired and dyslexic children is relevant here.

As Tallal et al., (1991, p. 369) point out:

> Specific elements of the acoustic signal within a phoneme are essential for perceptual discrimination. For example, steady-state vowels transmit the same acoustic information throughout their spectra. However, stop consonant-vowel syllables have a transitional period between the release of the consonant and the initiation of the vowel during which the frequencies change very rapidly in time.

The most basic factor in auditory processing is the duration of sound segments. Also crucial is the issue of the hierarchy in the sonority of the vowels and the enveloping consonants in syllable composition. In phonological theory, the sonority principle is specified as follows (Anderson and Ewen, 1987):

stop > fricative > nasal > liquid > semi-vowel > vowel

In the sonority scale, vowels are at the top, followed by semi-vowels, liquids, nasals, fricatives, and stops, in descending order. Acoustically, stops have the least energy and fricatives are noisy hissing sounds. Nasals and liquids (l and r) are consonantal as well as vocalic in feature composition. Then, the syllable is organized as follows:

(stop) + (fricative) + (nasal) + (liquid) + (semi-vowel) + (vowel)
(semi-vowel) + (liquid) + (nasal) + (fricative) + (stop)

The only known exception to the sonority generalization is Polish, which allows onsets with unusual consonantal combinations (Gussmann, 2002).

This is not a mystery if you consider how the different sounds are produced. When vowels are produced, the vocal tract is relatively open and the air from the lungs passes without any obstruction. The overall spectrum shape for a vowel is determined by the frequencies of the formants and by the spectrum of the glottal source (Stevens, 1998). This is the reason why vowels are called resonant sounds or steady-state sonorants. When the liquids l and r are produced, the air passes from the two sides of the tongue, that is the air passage is not fully open. The fricatives (f, v, s, sh, and the other hissing sounds) are produced when the air is obstructed at different places in the mouth. At the other extreme, stops require a complete blockage of the passing air at different places. They are produced when the mouth is opened; that is why they are also called plosives. On a spectograph, vowels are marked by formants and the presence of fricatives is marked by a lot of energy, while stops are just blanks.

Perhaps the usually ignored sound is the sound of silence, that is, "brief silent intervals of up to 200 msec duration, not longer pauses." (Repp, 1988.) He goes on to say:

> From an auditory perspective, silence is the absence of energy, a gap, an interruption that separates the signal portions to be perceived. In speech perception, however, silence is bridged by and participates in, integrative processes. Rather than being the neutral backdrop for the theater of auditory events, silence is informationally equivalent to energy-carrying signal portions. Relative duration of silence has been shown to be a cue for the perception of stop consonant voicing (Kohler, 1979; Lisker, 1957; Port, 1979), manner (Bailey and Summerfield, 1980; Repp, 1984; Liberman, Eccardt, and Pesetsky, 1978), and place of articulation (Bailey and Summerfield, 1980; Port, 1979; Repp, 1984) …. silence … is an integral part of the acoustic patterns that a human listener has learned to recognize (*ibid.*, p. 250).

The acoustics of sound composition is also reflected in neurophysiological processing. Phillips and Farmer (1990) look at the research findings on what is known as "acquired word deafness" in this context. Pure word deafness is a disorder of auditory discrimination specifically restricted to verbal stimuli. The adult patients with acquired word deafness and bilateral (in both the left and the right hemispheres) lesions of the primary auditory cortex can discriminate steady-state vowels, but they cannot discriminate consonants, in general, and stops, in particular. Phillips and Farmer reason that,

> The only sense in which a steady-state vowel has a time-structure that could be used as a basis for its discrimination is its time-waveform. The fact that vowel discrimination is largely unaffected in word deafness suggests that if humans distinguish vowels on the basis of their time structure, then auditory cortex makes little or no contribution to temporal discrimination of that grain.

On the other hand, if steady-state vowels are distinguished on the basis of the spectral structure, then the fact that their perception survives in word deafness offers no evidence on temporal processing, since they, by definition, have no temporal variations in spectral content. (*ibid.*, p. 88.)

Phillips and Farmer (*ibid.*) also point out that stop consonants have two levels of temporal organization: "The fine time-waveform, which has a grossly submillisecond grain, is one and it completely specifies the slower spectral changes that identify the consonant phonetically." Hence,

> ... the impairment of stop consonant discrimination in word deafness must reflect a temporal processing deficit in a time-frame that the stops possess but which the vowels do not, viz., one with a grain in the milliseconds to tens-of-milliseconds range, and one which happens to characterize the stops phonetically.

Interestingly, the damaged primary auditory cortex can process fricatives, nasals, and liquids to some extent. The reason offered by Phillips and Farmer (*ibid.*) is that the sounds fricatives, nasals, and liquids make are "often both longer in duration and less temporally differentiated than the stops."
The primary auditory cortex is not crucially involved in discriminations of the temporal grain. It is tonotopically organized. Its afferent pathway preserves the frequency-specific processing channels developed in the subcortical periphery as the cochlea's place code.

> The cortical representation of the spectral content of any given auditory event resides in the spatial distribution of activity evoked across the neural mosaic mapping the frequency organization of the cochlea. The temporal content of a sound is expressed in the temporal spacing between neural responses, since this will reflect the timing of events in the sound (*ibid.*, p. 90).

Also relevant and important is the difference in hemispheric mechanisms in the perception of steady-state vowels, semi-vowels, liquids, nasals, fricatives and stops. Cutting's (1974, p. 609) experiments suggest that sounds, which contain rapid changes in frequency, need special processing in the left hemisphere, even if the sounds are not classified as speech:

> A subsystem which tracks rapidly changing frequencies may not be needed in the right hemisphere which is geared for less highly analytical processing (Semmes, 1968). The notion of an independent transition analyzer in the left hemisphere is congruent with results of Darwin (1971). He found that fricatives with formant transitions yielded a right ear advantage, while the same fricatives without transitions yielded no advantage.

Interestingly, Cutting (*ibid.*) points out that the difference in hemispheric mechanisms for the cv and v stimuli "may be entirely attributable to the auditory, but not phonetic, analysis of stop consonants."

The acoustic–neurophysiological perspective on segmental sounds is important in understanding the developmental time-course underlying the concept of phonological awareness and its association with reading acquisition. It is equally relevant and critical in interpreting the diverse databases on dyslexic performance on the tasks involving phonological awareness, naming, and oral reading of regular words as well as regular nonsense strings.

In overview, it is clear that vowels, liquids, nasals, fricatives, and stops are different acoustically, both across and within the phonetic categories associated with them. They are also not processed by the same mechanisms, or the same hemisphere, or cortical-subcortical areas. The use of the concept "phonological" or "phonemic" awareness, the way it is operationalized in experimental research, and the role assigned to it in the natural proc ss of reading acquisition ignore this scientific scholarship.

Chapter Seven

STUDIES: LANGUAGE AND SCHOOL SYSTEMS

INTRODUCTION

For this investigation, three studies were carried out in Vadodara (formerly known as Baroda), which is a major city in the state of Gujarat in India. The first study in 1983 (Patel, 1995; Patel and Soper, 1987) was planned within the framework of standard research design and experimental statistics, especially from an integrated neuropsychological–psycholinguistic perspective. The next two studies done in 1997 and 1999 followed an exploratory approach. All three studies involved Gujarati-speaking children from the mainstream, mainly Hindu society, and its social–economic–cultural outskirts, the Scheduled Castes and Scheduled Tribes.

Gujarati is an Indo-European language with several dialects. The city of Vadodara is considered to be a part of the standard dialect area. Interestingly, the socioeconomically disadvantaged groups, especially those who provide services, living at the outskirts of the mainstream society in Vadodara, use the standard dialect of Gujarati. This is an important point to keep in mind when the performance of the children from these groups, called "scheduled" here, is considered.

Kiparsky (1979, p. 436) suggests that the canonical syllable type cv "enjoys the most favoured status in the languages of the world," which is true in the case of Gujarati. The cv syllable appears to be in the high frequency range in Gujarati:

word	syllables	gloss
nidhi	cv cv	a first name
ritu	cv cv	a first name
he ma	cv cv	a name
ma dhu ri	cv cv cv	a name
ʃuʂəma	cv cv cv	a first name
charuləta	cv cv cv cv	a first name
Sakahari	cv cv cv cv	vegetarian

According to Kiparsky, the syllable type vc is not so common in the known languages of the world. In Gujarati, the frequency of the v(c) type is low in specific word types:

word	syllables	gloss
ek	vc	one
əlka	vc cv	a first name
up kar	vc cvc	obligation
in di ra	vc cv cv	a first name
am li	vc cv	tamarind
əg ni	vc cv	fire

Finally, the syllable type vc(c) is rarely found.

word	syllables	gloss
əʂʈ	vcc	eight
əkʂər	vc cvc	orthographic unit
utpəla	vc cv cv	a first name
urmila	vc cv cv	a first name
əlpə	vc cv	small
əlpahar	vc cv cvc	breakfast or snack

The other syllable types in Gujarati consist of v, vv, cvc, cccv, cvcc, and cccvv:

word	syllables	gloss
uma	v cv	a first name
ushakant	v cv cvcc	a first name
maa laa	cvv cvv	garland
kəlp	cvcc	idea
shru ti	cccv cv	heard
drəu pə di	ccvv cv cv	a first name
stri	cccv	woman
indira	vc cv cv	a first name
kaur va ki	cvvc cv cv	a name
chəndrəmukhi	cvc ccv cv cv	a name

əkşərəs IN Gujarati

The Gujarati əkşərə can represent: v, vv, cv, ccv, cccv, and cccvv, and c (a postvocalic long consonant). There is however one exception which allows a vc or a cvc əkşərə: The *anusvara* (nasalization) in the postvocalic position is included in the əkşərə which makes it a cvc or a vc syllable in Gujarati. As Mistry (1996, p. 393) points out, *anusvara* in Gujarati has two values: either nasalization of a vowel or a nasal consonant homorganic with a following stop consonant.

word	syllables	əkşərəs	Gujarati *script*	gloss
aākh	vvcc	vvc c	આંખ	eye
rāg	cvc	vc c	રંગ	colour

It may be noted that the *anusvara* is the only postvocalic consonant that is included in an əkşərə in Gujarati and Devanagari. Recall, in general, əkşərəs don't allow any cvc or vc combinations. This exception disappears when the guidelines provided by the *Pratishakhya* scholars is taken into account. The *Pratishakhya* scholars considered both the vocalic and the consonantal processes in *anusvara* and preferred to emphasize the vocalic component in nasalization. Hence, the əkşərəs in the words *ankh* and *rang* would be vv and c.

The problem of the consonants following vowels in syllables like cvc and vc word-internally and at the end of words is interesting in *əkṣərə* formation. This is also an important issue in current phono-logical theory and models of syllable structure. Consider the following examples:

Word	Syllables	*əkṣərə*s
bekul	bə kul	bə ku l
bar	bar	ba r
chakər	cha kər	cha kə r
əlpə	əl pə	ə lpə
ərchənə	ər chə na	ə rchə na
əlka	əl ka	ə lka
eklo	ek lo	e k lo
chhokri	chhok ri	chho k ri
chərbi	chər bi	chə r bi

In the first set, the word-final consonant is given the status of an *əkṣərə*; the word-final syllable cvc is split up into cv and c. In word com-binations, the process of *sandhi* takes place and the word-final c gets integrated into the following onset, or takes the place of an onset for the following v. In the second set, the word-internal consonant is merged with the following onset. The examples in the third set raise an interesting issue.

The cvc is split into cv and c following the usual practice. However, the c is treated as a whole *matra* or a mora, which allows it the status of an *əkṣərə*. It seems that this word-internal consonant is followed by a brief but perceptually significant juncture, a sound of silence. The word /*khichdi*/ is not pronounced as /*khichədi*/in Gujarati, but it is written as /*khichədi*/. In Marathi, the spoken form corresponds with the written form /*khichədi*/.

The issue of the presence or absence of the schwa in the word-final and word-internal contexts in the different languages in India needs to be examined in relation to the phonetic–phonological principles underlying the different derivatives of Brāhmī.

GUJARATI *əkṣərə*s

ક કા કિ કી કુ કૂ કે કૈ કો કૌ કં કઃ
ખ ખા ખિ ખી ખુ ખૂ ખે ખૈ ખો ખૌ ખં ખઃ

ગ	ગા	ગિ	ગી	ગુ	ગૂ	ગે	ગૈ	ગો	ગૌ	ગં	ગઃ
ધ	ધા	ધિ	ધી	ધુ	ધૂ	ધે	ધૈ	ધો	ધૌ	ધં	ધઃ

Model 7.1 lists the Gujarati akṣərəs.

Model 7.1
Gujarati akṣərəs

ક	કા	કિ	કી	કુ	કૂ	કે	કૈ	કો	કૌ	કં	કઃ
ખ	ખા	ખિ	ખી	ખુ	ખૂ	ખે	ખૈ	ખો	ખૌ	ખં	ખઃ
ગ	ગા	ગિ	ગી	ગુ	ગૂ	ગે	ગૈ	ગો	ગૌ	ગં	ગઃ
ઘ	ઘા	ઘિ	ઘી	ઘુ	ઘૂ	ઘે	ઘૈ	ઘો	ઘૌ	ઘં	ઘઃ
ચ	ચા	ચિ	ચી	ચુ	ચૂ	ચે	ચૈ	ચો	ચૌ	ચં	ચઃ
છ	છા	છિ	છી	છુ	છૂ	છે	છૈ	છો	છૌ	છં	છઃ
જ	જા	જિ	જી	જુ	જૂ	જે	જૈ	જો	જૌ	જં	જઃ
ઝ	ઝા	ઝિ	ઝી	ઝુ	ઝૂ	ઝે	ઝૈ	ઝો	ઝૌ	ઝં	ઝઃ
ટ	ટા	ટિ	ટી	ટુ	ટૂ	ટે	ટૈ	ટો	ટૌ	ટં	ટઃ
ઠ	ઠા	ઠિ	ઠી	ઠુ	ઠૂ	ઠે	ઠૈ	ઠો	ઠૌ	ઠં	ઠઃ
ડ	ડા	ડિ	ડી	ડુ	ડૂ	ડે	ડૈ	ડો	ડૌ	ડં	ડઃ
ઢ	ઢા	ઢિ	ઢી	ઢુ	ઢૂ	ઢે	ઢૈ	ઢો	ઢૌ	ઢં	ઢઃ
ણ	ણા	ણિ	ણી	ણુ	ણૂ	ણે	ણૈ	ણો	ણૌ	ણં	ણઃ
ત	તા	તિ	તી	તુ	તૂ	તે	તૈ	તો	તૌ	તં	તઃ
થ	થા	થિ	થી	થુ	થૂ	થે	થૈ	થો	થૌ	થં	થઃ
દ	દા	દિ	દી	દુ	દૂ	દે	દૈ	દો	દૌ	દં	દઃ
ધ	ધા	ધિ	ધી	ધુ	ધૂ	ધે	ધૈ	ધો	ધૌ	ધં	ધઃ
ન	ના	નિ	ની	નુ	નૂ	ને	નૈ	નો	નૌ	નં	નઃ
પ	પા	પિ	પી	પુ	પૂ	પે	પૈ	પો	પૌ	પં	પઃ
ફ	ફા	ફિ	ફી	ફુ	ફૂ	ફે	ફૈ	ફો	ફૌ	ફં	ફઃ
બ	બા	બિ	બી	બુ	બૂ	બે	બૈ	બો	બૌ	બં	બઃ
ભ	ભા	ભિ	ભી	ભુ	ભૂ	ભે	ભૈ	ભો	ભૌ	ભં	ભઃ
મ	મા	મિ	મી	મુ	મૂ	મે	મૈ	મો	મૌ	મં	મઃ
ય	યા	યિ	યી	યુ	યૂ	યે	યૈ	યો	યૌ	યં	યઃ
ર	રા	રિ	રી	રુ	રૂ	રે	રૈ	રો	રૌ	રં	રઃ
લ	લા	લિ	લી	લુ	લૂ	લે	લૈ	લો	લૌ	લં	લઃ
વ	વા	વિ	વી	વુ	વૂ	વે	વૈ	વો	વૌ	વં	વઃ
શ	શા	શિ	શી	શુ	શૂ	શે	શૈ	શો	શૌ	શં	શઃ
ષ	ષા	ષિ	ષી	ષુ	ષૂ	ષે	ષૈ	ષો	ષૌ	ષં	ષઃ
સ	સા	સિ	સી	સુ	સૂ	સે	સૈ	સો	સૌ	સં	સઃ
ક્ષ	ક્ષા	ક્ષિ	ક્ષી	ક્ષુ	ક્ષૂ	ક્ષે	ક્ષૈ	ક્ષો	ક્ષૌ	ક્ષં	ક્ષઃ
જ્ઞ	જ્ઞા	જ્ઞિ	જ્ઞી	જ્ઞુ	જ્ઞૂ	જ્ઞે	જ્ઞૈ	જ્ઞો	જ્ઞૌ	જ્ઞં	જ્ઞઃ
હ	હા	હિ	હી	હુ	હૂ	હે	હૈ	હો	હૌ	હં	હઃ
ળ	ળા	ળિ	ળી	ળુ	ળૂ	ળે	ળૈ	ળો	ળૌ	ળં	ળઃ

There are some consonant conjuncts. For example,

જ્ઞ ક્ષ ત્ર શ્ર

In these conjuncts, the individual identities of the consonants cannot be seen. Interestingly, the *Pratishakhya* scholars treated these conjuncts as single units; hence they are represented as conjuncts in script topography. This is common in Devanagari and other related scripts.

Vowels as *akṣərə*s: **v and vv**

અ	આ	ઇ	ઈ	ઉ	ઊ	ઋ	એ	ઐ	ઓ	ઔ
ə	a	i	ii	u	uu	ṛ	e	əi	o	əu

ONGOING CHANGES IN
GUJARATI PHONOLOGY–ORTHOGRAPHY

There are some interesting changes taking place in Gujarati speech habits. Until recently, the *akṣərə* sign [ફ] was used to represent the aspirated voiceless bilabial stop [ph], which is quickly and selectively disappearing among Gujarati native speakers. The aspirated voiceless bilabial stop [ph] now occurs in three forms: (*a*) voiceless labiodental fricative [f]; (*b*) voiceless bilabial fricative [ɸ]; and, (*c*) aspirated voiceless bilabial stop [ph].

There are two additional changes in Gujarati phonology which some advocates of reform are using to force changes in orthography. The vocalic length for which there are different signs has been gradually neutralized: Long and short vowel signs in the Gujarati script are used only on the basis of standard dictionaries. The phonemic contrasts [s], [sh] and [ṣ] are also almost extinct and are also used in writing on the basis of dictionaries.

To recapitulate our understanding of how the orthographic unit *akṣərə* works in Gujarati, let me give you a list of words with their syllabic and *akṣərə* representations. This list shows how simple as well as complex *akṣərə*s are formed. Notice how resyllabification takes place when complex *akṣərə*s are formed. Remember that a consonant after a vowel in a cvc or a vc syllable which cannot reach the value of a whole *matra* or a mora is passes on to the onset position of the next syllable that follows in a word:

words	syllables	əkṣərəs	Gujarati *script*	*gloss*
buddhə	cvc cv	cv ccv	બુદ્ધ	Buddha
ashrəm	vc cvc	v ccv c	આશ્રમ	monastery
uvəṭ	v cvc	v cv c	ઉવટ	name
r̥gved	cvc cvc	cv c cv c	ઋગવેદ	Rgved
məmta	cvc cv	cv c cv	મમતા	feeling
chəula	cv v cv	cvv cv	ચૌલા	a first name

SCHOOLS IN VADODARA

As elsewhere in India, there are two Gujarati-medium school systems in actual practice in Vadodara. The different government bodies manage the public school system, while private schools belong to the sphere of free enterprise. The general education policy, including the school curriculum, is determined at the national level. The way it is put into practice depends upon the type of school system. There are also vast differences in teacher qualifications and the social–economic–cultural backgrounds of the pupils attending the two types of schools. There are, however, a few exceptions to this rule. For example, within the framework of the Hindu caste system, many people from the high castes, hence high social status, are poor and therefore cannot afford private schools.

The public schools are fully funded and controlled by the government bureaucracy. At the local municipal level, school boards manage teacher selections following the quota system, which gives preference to members of specified disadvantaged groups. These include mainly people from the Scheduled Castes and Tribes. The pupils in public schools are homogeneous, albeit mostly in one respect: They primarily come from the lower socioeconomic groups, which also, by and large, belong to the Scheduled Castes and Tribes. Their profile is clearly indicated by where their parents live, that is, at the outskirts of the mainstream residential areas. The profile of the public school pupil varies with respect to intelligence, motivation, and attitude toward education. They are also deeply conscious of the fact that they belong to the public school system and perhaps more importantly, to the Scheduled Castes and Tribes.

The private school system is very different from the public school system in every way. Middle-class parents sacrifice a great deal to get their sons and daughters admitted to a private school with a good academic reputation. The private school children consider themselves superior to the pupils in public schools. Their parents also take serious interest in their children's work habits and progress.

The most conspicuous educational phenomenon in Vadodara, common to other cities in India too, is the English-medium school. This private enterprise is growing at a fast rate to meet the increasing demand for it. The pupils in this educational system may be described as native speakers of Indian English. This type of schooling is creating a whole new linguistic–cultural group who feel increasingly out of touch with the millions who really experience the realities of life in India. For my purpose, this school system is not relevant and is, thus, not included in the studies described in this book.

The most striking phenomenon in the Indian educational system is private tuition classes, which have burgeoned to such an extent that it obviates the regular educational system, specifically in the private sector. The operators responsible for this system are teachers with effective teaching skills and enormous physical stamina to work before and after school hours. They work long hours for big incomes and move around like Bollywood celebrities. Amazingly, even some public school children from scheduled groups pay some individuals in their neighborhoods to get help with their schoolwork. This is not common, and most of these tutors are housewives with some education trying to find extra income.

TEACHING OF READING

Currently, the policy makers at the national level recommend what is known as the whole language approach, which is a rival of the phonics approach in North America and New Zealand. In this approach, teachers and pupils are not supposed to begin with decoding which requires, in India, the introduction of the *varnamala* and *akṣarə*s. Even so, the majority of teachers begin with the *varnamala*. Usually, the *varnamala* is recited as a matter of routine by the whole class in grade one. It is done very rhythmically and melodiously. In most classrooms, the walls have *varnamala* tables which the pupils see all the time. There are also such tables for basic and complex *akṣarə*s on the classroom walls. In some schools, teachers prepare very creative diagrams too.

In the pedagogical approach, it is important to note that complex *akṣarə*s are not explained in terms of their vowel and consonant constituents until the fifth grade. For the pupils, the *akṣarə*s are whole units. For example, they are unaware that the *akṣarə* for /stri/ consists of /s/, /t/, /r/, and /i/. Some children arrive at this type of awareness on their own and perhaps on the basis of guidance from parents and siblings. But as a matter of classroom pedagogy, this type of teaching is delayed until grade five in both private and public Gujarati-medium schools. What happens in the case of the multitude of children who attend English-medium schools is an interesting research question.

PUPIL PROFILE

With just a few exceptions, the student population as a whole is impressively quiet, polite, and nonviolent. Their schoolbags contain books and pencils. By and large, they show enormous respect toward their teachers; the teachers in turn demand it and some achieve it through hand slaps. The attitude of the majority of pupils towards education is positive. The children in private as well as public schools are quite original and idealistic in their career goals and are quite unlike their parents who are actually very practical and want their children to become either computer scientists, corporate executives, or medical specialists. These ambitious parents belong mainly to the middle- or upper-middle-class socioeconomic groups. They are equally ferocious in getting their children married following the new caste–class commercial modes, which would make their Vedic ancestors sick. Some Scheduled Caste girls told me that they would like to follow in the footsteps of "Bapu" (Mohandas Karamchand Gandhi) and serve the nation.

Chapter Eight

CHILDREN FROM MAINSTREAM GROUPS

STUDY I

Study I was conducted in 1983 (June–August) at the beginning of the school year, which coincides with the monsoon season in Vadodara, Gujarat (for background and detailed accounts of the study, see Patel, 1995; Patel and Soper, 1987). The study was planned under the shadow of the experience I acquired in conducting the research that has formed the basis of the book *Reading Disabilities: The Interaction of Reading, Language, and Neuropsychological Deficits* (Doehring et al., 1981). This study looked at "specific reading disability" or "developmental dyslexia" in order to examine intact and deficient psycholinguistic processes and neuropsychological mechanisms in relation to the different deficient reading skills.

The domain of writing systems and reading acquisition began to attract attention at this time. In this context, I began to think about the Gujarati script, especially the formation of əkṣərəs. The article by Scheerer-Neumann (1981) was influential in my thinking; this study demonstrated that poor readers were helped by "intraword structure," that is, spacing of syllables in words. I realized that this facility was built into the way əkṣərəs were sequenced in Gujarati words.

As a result of the focus on "specific deficits" in different syndromes and definitions based on "exclusionary criteria" in neuropsychology, only "otherwise normal children" were selected as subjects. In the case of developmental dyslexia, the subjects were supposed to be deficient only in reading acquisition. Since their intelligence was in the average and above average range, failure in learning to read was considered "unexpected." Children who faced "the cycles of disadvantage," that is, below average intelligence, low socioeconomic status, crowded housing, and psychological problems (Rutter and Madge, 1976) were excluded from subject samples. Given this methodological logic, I selected Alembic School, a prestigious private school with both Gujarati-medium and English-medium sections.

SUBJECTS

A total of 120 Gujarati-speaking children in this school, 40 each from the first month of grades two, three, and four, were selected. According to teachers' reports, all the children showed regular achievement in reading, writing, and arithmetic. The age range was from seven to nine years, which is supposed to be an important period for the acquisition of literacy skills (Doehring, 1976). Even though most of the children in this school were upper-middle and middle-class with socioeconomic as well as cultural advantages, there were some children whose parents had to struggle to survive. These children were admitted because their fathers worked for the company which owned the school or because their parents managed to find a connection to some senior teacher or the principal.

TESTS

This was the first experimental study conducted in Gujarati to test specific hypotheses regarding psycholinguistic processes in reading and spelling acquisition. All the test materials were experimenter-made, hence, not standardized. All the primary and secondary reading primers actually used by the children in grades one to four were checked in great detail. The words and paragraphs selected for the different tests were ecologically valid, in that they were taken from grades one to four basic and secondary textbooks.

The reading skills tested involved: (*a*) **oral word reading** (40 words, 10 each from the textbooks of grades one to four); (*b*) **word comprehension** (word-picture matching, 40 words, 10 each from the first four grades); and, (*c*) **paragraph comprehension** (paragraph-picture matching, 20 items, 5 each from the first four grades).

Orthographic parsing (segmentation) was tested at two levels: (*a*) akṣərə, and (*b*) phoneme (10 items in each category). Children were shown familiar written words and they were required to orally delete a graphemic sign for either an akṣərə or a phonemic segment (from an akṣərə). The written visual aid was provided so that the unit to be deleted could be pointed out by the experimenter.

Morphographic recognition, that is, the ability to recognize morphemes in written words, was also assessed by showing written words (10 items) parsed (segmented) three ways, one showing a morphemic parsing and the other two with random segmentations.

The **spelling test** consisted of three components: **regular, analogical**, and **nonsense** words (20 items in each category). Analogical spelling was assessed through stimuli which were constructed from regular words by changing the grapheme in the initial position (e.g., /badhuri/ for /madhuri/, /buhi/ for /juhi/, and /bandey/ for /pandey/ (see Campbell, 1983). This is similar to a Gujarati speech game in which all the words beginning with the sound /b/, that is, the first phoneme is replaced with /b/; hence, the task was not totally novel to the subjects. The third spelling task, nonsense spelling, consisted of stimuli composed of randomly arranged akṣərəs; these akṣərəs could not be rearranged to form regular words.

PROCEDURE

The subjects were tested in a quiet room; at times, some children passing by peeped through the windows with a great deal of curiosity. All testing was conducted individually except for the spelling assessments, which were administered in groups of eight. Words for spelling were dictated by a research assistant who was a native speaker of standard Gujarati and a graduate student in psychology. The stimuli were presented with consistent articulation and time intervals. Instructions and practice were given for all the nine tests.

MAJOR RESULTS:
TRENDS IN LEARNING TO READ GUJARATI

Of obvious interest is the pattern of results on **orthographic parsing** at the phonemic, *akṣara*, and morpheme levels. Test scores on phonemic parsing were not different for grades two and three; the scores for grade four were significantly higher. All the mean scores on parsing at the phonemic level were low: 4.23, 4.25, and 6.45 out of 10. As expected, performance on *akṣara* parsing was significantly higher at the three grade levels: 7.60, 9.53, and 8.78 out of 10. The range of individual differences in phoneme and *akṣara* parsing was almost non-existent. In other words, the poor performance in phonemic parsing was common, that is, there were no subjects who showed superior performance. Similarly, there were no subjects who performed extremely poorly in *akṣara* parsing. The scores on orthographic parsing at the morphemic level were poor for the three groups: 5.50, 5.38, and 5.50 out of 10; interestingly, there was a wide range in variability among subjects within each grade.

The test scores on **oral word reading** and **word comprehension** were high at all the grade levels without any marked individual differences within each grade. Grades two and three again performed at the same level; grade four, showed a substantial improvement. Similarly, children in grades two and three obtained similar scores on **paragraph comprehension**; there was a significant rise in scores at the grade four level. However, response time decreased at each higher grade level.

The performance on **oral word reading**, **word comprehension** and **paragraph comprehension** showed very similar patterns in development. More than 90 percent of the children performed well on three-quarters or more of the test items. What is striking is that even children beginning grade two obtained high scores on oral word reading. This particular result clearly suggests that these children can transform *akṣaras* into sound units after just one year of classroom time. Interestingly, these children at the beginning of grade two were not just decoding the print; they could also make sense of written words and paragraphs. The high scores on oral word reading, word comprehension, and paragraph comprehension were opposed to the low scores on these children's ability to parse written words at the phonemic and morphemic levels. On the other hand, parsing at the level of the *akṣara* was acquired easily and mastered by grade three. To put it simply, success in oral word reading and paragraph comprehension was not hampered by the inability to segment *akṣara*s into their phonemic parts. What was important for these children in learning to read words orally and comprehend paragraphs was that they could recognize *akṣara*s as whole units.

Scores on the regular spelling task gradually improved over the grades, but only the difference between grades two and four was significant. In the case of analogical spelling, there was a significant improvement in grades two and three, but only a small further improvement in grade four. The performance on nonsense spelling falls into the pattern observed for oral word reading, word comprehension, paragraph comprehension, and phonemic parsing; that is, it improves only after grade three.

Given the pattern of the results on oral word reading, word comprehension, phonemic parsing, and nonsense spelling, the correlations derived both for the subject population and within each grade give a clear message. Phonemic parsing scores were found to be unrelated to oral word reading, word comprehension, and nonsense spelling. The highest correlations with the oral word reading task for grades two, three, and four accounted for only 3 percent of the variance. This finding is particularly critical since the oral word reading, word comprehension, and nonsense spelling scores follow the same format of no change over grades two and three, and improvement in grade four.

However, the scores in grade two on oral word reading, word comprehension, and nonsense spelling were interrelated. This appeared to be primarily attributable to the performances in grade two. By grade three only oral word reading and word comprehension were related, and by grade four there appeared to be effectively no relationship between oral word reading, word comprehension, and nonsense spelling.

Gujarati-speaking children in grades two, three, and four achieved high scores in oral word reading, word comprehension, and paragraph comprehension. On the other hand, their performances vis-à-vis phonemic and morphemic parsing were poor. The scores on orthographic parsing at the phonemic and morphemic levels were not correlated with oral word reading, word comprehension, and paragraph comprehension. It can be safely said that the ability to parse written words at the phonemic and morphemic levels played no apparent role in reading acquisition in this case.

What arouses one's curiosity is the ease with which Gujarati-speaking children acquire and master the ability to parse written words at the level of *akṣarəs* by grade three. The results show, effectively, no correlation between performance on this task and those involving the reading skills, namely, oral word reading, word comprehension, and paragraph comprehension at any level. The relationship between *akṣarə* parsing and word comprehension approaches significance at grade four, but it accounts for only 8 percent of the variance. No other correlation accounts for more than 1 percent of the variance.

The correlations between the regular, the analogical, and the nonsense spelling scores showed interesting patterns. Scores on regular and analogical spelling were related at both grade two and grade four, but not at grade three. In fact, the correlation at grade three was significantly lower than that at either grade two or grade four. Regular and nonsense spelling were related at grade two and grade three, but not at grade four, although none of the differences between these correlations were significant.

In terms of regular spelling in grade two, the relationships observed in Gujarati-speaking children might suggest that both lexical storage and written–spoken correspondences play important roles; it may also be inferred that for both analogical and regular spelling the written–spoken correspondences play the most important role. Since the relationship between analogical and nonsense spelling is quite high at grade three, the latter interpretation seems more appropriate. By grade three, nonsense and regular spelling indicated a relationship, suggesting that written–spoken correspondences still play a major role.

The lack of a relationship between nonsense and analogical spelling at grade three suggests that orthographic lexical storage is being formed and used when more appropriate. By grade four, the mental lexical storage appears to be the most important, and there is little relationship between nonsense spelling and either regular or analogical spelling. The results for the *akṣarǝ* parsing task also appear to reflect this change. The grade four performance on this task, while superior to that of grade two, was inferior to that of grade three. Using the orthographic lexical storage for normal spelling may facilitate this task, but it would initially be disruptive on a relatively novel task in which the written–spoken unit correspondence schemas may be of primary importance.

How about a comparison of the relative changes in performance over grades two, three, and four on the three spelling tasks? Since a different dependent variable is involved in each task, a direct comparison cannot be justified. Also, across all the three grades the nonsense spelling scores clearly show poorer performance than the other spelling scores. However, by performing transformations on the regular spelling scores through the linear regression equations derived between the two pairs of spelling scores (regular and analogical, regular and nonsense) for all subjects ($N = 120$), an insight into the relative grade performance can be gained. When doing so for grade two, the analogical spelling scores fall below the transformed regular spelling scores, but the nonsense spelling scores do not. The nonsense spelling scores still do not differ significantly from the transformed regular spelling scores in grade three. Now the analogical and transformed regular scores do not differ either. By grade four, the transformed scores reflect less improvement in regular spelling compared to grades two and three than in either analogical or nonsense spelling. This particular differential rate of relative change in performance on these tasks further supports the hypothesis of a change in the processes used for regular spelling. (For all the statistical information, see the original paper by Patel and Soper, 1987.)

Chapter Nine

Children from Scheduled Groups Living in Outer Areas

Introduction

Both in terms of test materials and methodology, this study moved away in significant ways from the previous one, which was cast in the standard experimental framework. After the first study (Patel and Soper, 1987), I decided to probe into specific reading processes mainly in children whose parents lived on the outskirts of mainstream society. These children are referred to as "children from scheduled groups" here. The parents of these children belong to low castes and tribal groups.

Methodological Caveat

My 1983 experience in empirical work with school children in India fuelled my interest in Edmund Coleman's (1981) emphasis on calibration. As Coleman argues, "... the very nature of the contemporary experiment and its statistical model almost guarantees that the findings will not be generalizable beyond the fixed-effect restrictions of laboratory paradigms." The cultural background of each educational system varies considerably. The attitude of teachers, parents, and the pupils toward education, in general, and experimental testing, in particular, plays an influential role in research outcomes. All the culture-specific variables are of particular importance when studying reading processes, especially in India, in view of its ancient tradition of recitation and the structure of the Hindu caste system.

At this stage in my academic growth, I was also ready to embrace David Rubin's (1989) arguments against experimental control and external validity in research designs. Since I could talk to the children in the study with a high degree of success, as I am familiar with their background and can speak Gujarati natively, I decided that the most productive strategy would be to look for trends in processual development in reading acquisition. Hence, even though I shall not overlook the basic tenets of scientific inquiry, I prefer to examine the relevant patterns emerging from the data without formulating null research hypotheses and trying to reject them statistically. It turned out that each subject was an individual unit and not just one subject in a selected group.

Study II

Study II was conducted in 1997. It consisted of two parts. The tests were first administered to a similar group of five children randomly selected from a different private school (Experimental School, M.S. University of Baroda) as a trial run for test items and tasks.

The first part consisted of a sample of children from a private school with a good academic reputation (Alembic School). A group of 16 children from grade three (nine years old) were given the new tests as a measure of "calibration" rather than as an experimental control. The process of "calibration" is used to ensure accuracy in instrumental measurements. Let us take the example of those instruments which pick up neural electrical responses to acoustic stimuli. Evoked potentials are electrical changes in the brain that are evoked by a stimulus; they are recordings made through macroelectrodes. When a signal is introduced into the ear, it passes through several way stations—the inner ear, the inferior colliculus in the brain stem, the medial geniculate nucleus in the thalamus, the primary auditory center (Heschl's gyrus), and the superior temporal lobe. These are the different processing stations located hierarchically in the auditory pathway between the ears and the cortex. It is established that the early auditory evoked responses that occur in 10 ms originate in the brain stem. Evoked responses, which occur after 10 and 50 ms are associated with the primary auditory center and the areas in the superior temporal lobe, respectively. All the different instruments involved in the operation must function appropriately when they are attached to the subjects one by one to make sure that the measurements and the numbers are accurate.

The procedure of calibration is also necessary for psycholinguistic tests expected to tap cognitive processes. Calibration in cognitive experiments takes care of the suitability of the test stimuli, tasks, and procedure vis-à-vis the subjects. The application of the theory of test scores looks at numbers, and not at subjects in the actual testing situation. In a standard experiment, the control group is compared with an experimental group to find significant differences using statistical procedures. The different experimental designs and statistical techniques are marvellous instruments when the required conditions can be fulfilled. The concept of experimental control assumes and requires complicated conditions regarding the suitability of subjects, stimuli, tasks, and procedures. Unless the test results can be replicated using different subjects, different stimuli, and different tasks, the results, especially in relation to language use, cannot be generalized.

The second part of this study included pupils from two public schools located in two different areas, one urban, and the other, urban–rural (Laxmipura, a village in the vicinity of Vadodara). A sizeable number of the children attending these schools did not know their ages and the school records were educated guesses. Not a single child had the advantage of the Vedic oral tradition, which is easily available to the children from mainstream Hindu society. They did not have any opportunity to attend a ceremony or a ritual at home or in the community where they could hear recitations in Sanskrit or listen to the professional reading of the epics Ramayana and Mahabharata. Not a single child could recite a poem from memory.

Since the roads leading to the urban–rural school site were blocked because of the monsoon, we could test only four children from grade three and one child from grade five. These children were between the ages of eight and 14 years. The grade three children did not seem to be ready for the tests even though they were selected by their teachers as the best from that grade level. The child from grade five was not very different from his younger counterparts.

The urban area school (Fateh Gunj, Vadodara) was accessible, though the entrance was often blocked by muddy water. Here too we were unsuccessful in testing grade three children. These children talked about what was going on in terms of their own progress and school situations. We moved on to grade five children and tested 16 of them, most of whom were almost regular in attendance.

The unhygienic condition of the school compound, especially during the rainy season, needs comment. In this school there was no lavatory for female students. Children were given lunch, but the sitting arrangement and the mess after the event, simply cannot be imagined by those who have not witnessed the situation. Keeping my nauseous feeling aside, I need to emphasize the high degree of toxicity in the environment in which these children were given their lunch. I shall return to the issue in the context of the toxicogenic conditions in which most of these children are raised when I discuss the question of whether the children from scheduled groups who read badly can be called "poor readers" or "dyslexics."

TESTS

1. **Picture Naming:** Ten familiar items were selected from each of the four categories of objects, birds, fruit, and flowers. The pictures of these items were pasted on cards. The pictures were cut out from popular posters, which are sold in the market as educational tools.
2. **Symbol Recognition:** Fifteen designs of nonsense objects were hand-drawn on cards. Each card contained three symbols, one of which was the target. The children were shown a symbol on a card and asked to examine the card in front of them. The task was to say "yes" or "no" to the question: "Is this picture on this card? Show it to me." Essentially, the task required visual target search and matching.
3. **Objects in Spatial Relations (On/Under/Left/Right/):** This test was a modification of the experimental task designed by Landau (1993). Nonsense objects were hand-drawn and given

names; the objects were totally unfamiliar to the local children and the names sounded like nonsense names. These pictures were placed on/under/to the left/to the right/of a hand-drawn table. The instruction was as follows: "Look, this is Lordes. Tell me if Lordes is under the table in this picture. Just say yes or no."

4. **Oral Repetition of Words:** Thirty familiar regular words consisting of three, four, and five *akşarə*s (10 in each of the three categories) were selected. Thirty nonsense words following the same pattern were created.

5. **Oral Reading of Regular and Nonsense Words—Basic and Complex *akşarə*s:** A total of 30 words, half with basic and the other half with complex *akşarə*s were selected from elementary grades textbooks. Thirty nonsense words, half with basic and the other half with complex *akşarə*s were created.

6. **Spelling:** The pattern for the oral word reading task was followed in this test. Thirty new regular words were selected and 30 new nonsense words were created. These words were dictated, individually, to each child.

7. **Rhyming—Odd Word Out:** Children were presented with groups of three words, two of which rhymed (for a total of 15 items). The task was to order the odd word out.

8. **Identification of Phonemes in *akşarə*s:** The children were shown cards (in total 15) with written *akşarə*s and they were asked to identify a given vowel or a consonant by pointing to it. The instruction was: "Show me the /u/ in this *akşarə* /pu/." All 15 items were basic *akşarə*s.

9. **Blending (Synthesis):** The children were orally presented with two parts of a word (for a total of 15 items) and were asked to blend the two and form words. The task basically involved complex *akşarə*s with consonant clusters.

10. **Visual *akşarə* Matching:** This task was similar to symbol matching. The cards (15 in total) contained *akşarə*s instead of nonverbal meaningless symbols.

11. **Visual Word Matching:** In this test, *akşarə*s were replaced with words (15 item in total).

The tests can be divided into four blocks: A–1, 2, 3, 4; B–5, 6; C–7, 8, 9; D–10, 11. Except for the A Block, which consists of a set of four tests involving very different and unrelated abilities, the other three blocks consisted of tests involving related abilities. The tests in Blocks B and C are based on psycholinguistic processes, which are considered crucial in reading acquisition research. Block D consists of tests related to *akṣərə* and word matching as visual units.

Symbol matching, a nonverbal visual process, was selected to correspond with visual *akṣərə* matching and visual word matching which involve orthographic structure at the level of the *akṣərə* and the word. Similarly, oral word reading of regular and nonsense words and spelling are to be interpreted in relation to rhyming, phoneme identification in *akṣərəs*, blending, and visual *akṣərə*–word matching.

The tests involving oral repetition and spatial relations processing for comprehension were selected with "developmental dyslexia" in mind. How these abilities can be interpreted in terms of developmental dyslexia, especially its neurobiological and psycholinguistic correlates, is discussed in Chapter 12.

MAJOR TRENDS IN RESULTS: MAINSTREAM CHILDREN IN A PRIVATE SCHOOL

All 16 children formed a homogeneous mainstream group so far as their performance on all the 11 tests is concerned. Surprisingly, the range of variability is marginal in the test scores of all the tests. The tests in which all the children showed an extremely high or almost zero level of achievement are remarkably separable. In other words, the abilities and processes underlying the two groups of tests are clearly disassociated. Given the results of Study I, this distinct division in reading processes is not surprising.

All 16 children almost reached the ceiling in Block A, that is, the group as a whole indicated a surprisingly high level of development in the abilities and processes underlying naming, nonverbal symbol recognition, grasp of spatial relations in language use, and oral repetition of very complex long words consisting of five *akṣərəs* with and without meaning. This can be taken as a sign of adequate general cognitive–linguistic development.

The tests in Block B, which require oral reading of words made up of basic and complex (consonant clusters) *akṣərəs* with and without meaning, revealed a similar pattern. The occasional errors were random or accidental in nature. The performance in the spelling of dictated words, which were equally complex in akṣara formation, was equally superb.

The tests in Block D followed the same trend. All of the 16 children succeeded with the same high level of performance in matching written akṣaras and words.

The pattern of superior performance in Blocks A, B, and D was not supported in the case of the Block C tests, which included rhyming, identifying the phonemic components in akṣaras, and blending, specifically words involving consonant clusters. Rhyming and blending stood apart from phoneme identification in akṣaras: In these tests there was considerable variability in scores, that is, the range in scores was wide. It seemed that most of the children found the tasks rather odd. It was interesting that almost all the children were unaware of rhyming as an activity.

The most strikingly negative pattern in scores emerged in the test which required subjects to break up the akṣaras, that is, consider the akṣaras as units made up of consonants and vowels. All 16 children singularly viewed akṣaras as whole units. In spite of their superior achievement in oral reading of regular and nonsense words as well as in akṣara and word matching, this group of children, without a single exception, failed to see the phonemic components in akṣaras. The task is ecologically strange. Parents and older siblings at home do not indulge in splitting up akṣaras into their component elements. A revealing explanation came from class teachers in two private schools. The pedagogy of akṣara formation and analysis begins in grade five when reading becomes almost a natural act for children. Grade five children in private schools read the primary as well as the secondary textbooks with ease and a sense of enjoyment. It is when they can carry out the process of reading simple and compound words made up of basic and complex akṣaras that children are taught to explicitly recognize the phonemic composition of akṣaras.

The mainstream children in grade three attending private schools showed impressively high levels of achievement in oral reading of regular as well as nonsense words, in spelling, in repetition of complex words, and in comprehension of spatial relations. All children were equally proficient in matching written akṣaras and words. The tests involving rhyme and blending presented a challenge for these third graders, and the test, which required the partition of phonemic components of akṣaras, simply baffled or floored them.

Knowing the pattern of achievement observed in the mainstream children attending a private school, we can now direct our attention to the children from scheduled groups who attend public schools. These are the children whose parents live in isolated ghettos at the outskirts of the mainstream residential areas.

CHILDREN FROM SCHEDULED GROUPS IN PUBLIC SCHOOLS

The test performance of children from scheduled groups in public schools attending grade three provided an interesting portrait, which highlighted their uniqueness in comparison to their counterparts from the mainstream in private schools. These four grade three children attending a public school in an urban–rural area were comfortable only in naming familiar objects, in their comprehension of spatial relations, and in symbol (nonverbal) recognition.

It must be noted that some children in the scheduled groups were raised in the Islamic tradition. They also attended an Islamic school where they were taught Urdu and the Perso-Arabic script and how to write it. Urdu is a sister language of Hindi with a large Persian vocabulary. The Persian component in their vocabulary was reflected in naming responses; that is, these Islamic children used Persian words to name several familiar objects, birds, flowers, etc. Since the Urdu script is read from the right to the left, the children with Islamic tutoring experienced a direction problem. For example, they read 71 as 17, and some of them did not recognize them as numbers, but as individual letters.

Their performance in naming familiar animals, birds, fruits, vegetables, etc., was not at the same level as that exhibited by children from the mainstream in private schools. Their correct responses often involved nonstandard words used by their communities, which were accepted by the researcher cheerfully. In visual nonverbal symbol matching they showed signs of success, but they could not do the same in the case of visual *akṣara* and word matching. They did well on the tests, which required comprehension of spatial relations and oral repetition of complex words and, obviously, enjoyed both. On all other tests, which involved processes related to word reading, they felt miserable and utterly helpless.

The child in grade five was superior to his younger mates only in naming, comprehension of spatial relations, nonverbal symbol recognition, oral word repetition, and to a lesser extent, in rhyming (picking the odd word out). So far as the processes related to word reading were concerned, this 12-year-old boy was not ahead of his grade three counterparts.

The 16 children from scheduled groups in grade five, attending an urban public school, were similar to the mainstream third graders so far as the patterns in test performance are concerned. Identifying the phonemic components in akṣərəs, recognizing rhyming words, and blending presented the same problems for these children from scheduled groups in grade five. With some exceptions, the tests involving naming and matching of written akṣərəs and words were not difficult. The ease with which the children from scheduled groups showed excellent performance in complex word repetition and comprehension of spatial relations was remarkable.

Most striking in the total pattern in the data on these children attending public schools is their performance in oral reading of regular and nonsense words. There was a high degree of homogeneity in this group in the way they ignored the vowel signs in initial as well as noninitial positions in akṣərəs: They recognized most of the consonants and pronounced them as if they were independent sounds. It seemed as if they were unaware of the way these sounds formed words.

How about the ability of children from scheduled groups to acquire spelling? The picture is not different in the test performance in spelling dictation. Out of the 16 children, only five could write some high frequency familiar words. What is interesting is that these children could use some vowel signs, which they could not decode in oral word reading. However, most of the words did not look like regular words. Here again, it seems reasonable to speculate that the concept of lexicality was out of reach for these children.

How do the children from scheduled groups compare with their brothers and sisters from the mainstream in their efforts to acquire some processes and skills to deal with written language? In general cognitive–linguistic development, they appear to be almost at par with their mainstream counterparts. However, when they are confronted with the written form of language, they are markedly behind in achievement. The most insurmountable obstacle for these children from scheduled groups is the relationship between spoken and written akṣərəs and words. The locus of this difficulty seems to involve the nature of vowels as sounds and their written signs. They can decode consonants in words as if they were single isolated elements which have nothing to do with the words in their mental dictionary.

Several studies indicate that English-speaking children who read poorly in North America misread vowels in oral word reading. It is suggested that, in English alphabetic spelling, the pronunciation of a given vowel depends upon its orthographic neighborhood. Hence, the question of vowel misreading in English words is explained in terms of the irregularity in vowel grapheme–phoneme correspondence rules by most researchers (Bryson and Werker, 1989; Fowler et al., 1977; Fowler et al., 1979; Werker et al., 1989).

As for consonant recognition in oral word reading, Werker et al., (1989) and Bryson and Werker (1989) suggest that the children who scored poorly in oral word reading added new consonants when they tried to pronounce nonsense words. Werker et al.'s (1989) analysis of consonant errors in oral word reading in their data based on Canadian children, the Roman alphabet, and English orthography suggests that disabled readers consistently add consonants when attempting to read nonsense words. The consonant error data on children who were normal readers shows that they made more phonetic feature substitutions than any other error type, that is, omissions and sequencing errors.

Within this framework of research, Zinna et al., (1986) studied the effect of word frequency upon the way children read English words with vowel digraphs. They asked first-, third-, and fifth-grade children from a school in Connecticut to read aloud high- and low-frequency words containing vowel digraph units with variant and invariant pronunciation. A significant main effect for word frequency for the first-, third-, and fifth-grade children was observed. Zinna et al. (*ibid.*, p. 471) suggest that "children's accuracy in word reading would be enhanced by high word frequency, regardless of the number of alternate pronunciations for the vowel digraph unit contained within these words." Moreover, the consistency of orthographic neighborhoods helps these children to read even low frequency words "with a level of accuracy close to that obtained for both high-frequency words and those of low frequency that contained invariant vowel digraph units" (p. 477). Since word frequency is an important variable in lexical processing, this observation regarding the importance of word frequency may suggest that the organization of the mental lexicon is implicated in children with problems in reading acquisition.

The question of irregularity in phonemic–graphemic correspond- ence rules does not arise in the case of Gujarati *akṣərə*s, and the fifth- grade children in the study simply ignored the vowels. The vowel signs have the same values, that is, the pronunciation of a given vowel does not depend upon its orthographic neighborhood. The phenomenon of vowel omission also cannot be accounted for in terms of the distinc- tion between visual shapes for initial and noninitial positions of vowels in words, which may appear to be a problem area in terms of popular common sense.

Another equally important difference noticed in the public school children from scheduled groups was that they did not add consonants when they tried to pronounce nonsense or regular words like their North American counterparts. They substituted some consonants, but these substitutions were related to the ongoing sociolinguistic changes in Gujarati phonology. For example, the distinction between /s/ and /sh/ has disappeared in everyday language use. This phenomenon is reflected in the children's substitution of /s/ for /sh/.

Perhaps the explanation of the way the children from scheduled groups ignored vowel signs and did not add consonants in oral word reading involves the developmental mechanisms responsible for stor- age and retrieval of words from the mental dictionary. The way these fifth-grade children read words aloud can be described as a hesitant and halting decoding of consonants, as if they were isolated sound units. There was no hint of any kind to suggest that the children were dealing with words. It seemed that the concept of lexicality evaded these children. These fifth-grade outlier children could not read words aloud even though the clues provided by the consonant sequences could have helped them to retrieve the phonological form of these words from the mental lexicon. For example, the consonant sequence /n-sh-l/ could be enough information for the search and retrieval pro- cesses to lead to the word /nishal/ ("school"). Whether the research findings on the developmental changes in American children's word recognition processes considered by Metsala and Walley (1998) can be replicated with the children from scheduled groups and the main- stream in India is an interesting question.

Most striking in the test performance of the children from scheduled groups are the signs of their ability to match written *akṣərə*s and words. Since these children were not poor in naming pictures, it may involve some specific problems related to the development and storage of their orthographic lexicon or images.

The case of an eight-year-old girl from a scheduled group in the third grade in the same public school must be noted. I have no doubt that this young lady in grade three can top the performance of all the mainstream third graders in private schools. I spotted this young lady from among a group of kids who tried to peek through the window of the room where the testing was being conducted. Since I was done for the day, I asked her if she would like to be tested. She readily agreed and amazed me with her performance in all the tests. She scored 100 percent in regular and nonsense word reading and she could easily parse *akṣarəs* into their consonant and vowel constituents. When I asked her about her career goal, she said she would like to be a doctor, a specialist. She added that her mother stayed home and her elder sister helped her with her schoolwork.

Chapter Ten

Children from Scheduled Groups Living in and around Upper-class Areas

Study III

Study III is different in two ways: The children tested in Study II came from scheduled groups who lived in outer areas ridden with highly unhygienic and toxic environmental conditions. In Study III, the children attended a public school in the area where their parents lived in "servants quarters" (mostly tents) of the upper-class residences or ghettoes not far from this area.

These children from scheduled groups played with the children from the mainstream and were not exposed, systematically, to toxins like their counterparts whose parents lived in isolated ghettoes. An observation of these children at play with the mainstream children gave the impression that the children from the scheduled groups forgot that their parents belonged to the lowest level of the Hindu caste system which stratifies people into hierarchically ordered cells. The restraints imposed by the caste system have no legal basis in present-day India, but its cultural legitimacy is deeply embedded in the Hindu psyche.

More tests were also developed to understand the problem of word reading in children from scheduled groups. In Study II, it was noticed that many children could match written *akṣaras* and words, even though they could not read them orally. In Study III, I added written word matching with spoken words and pictures, and paragraph comprehension.

THE SCHOOL (VADIVADI IN ALKAPURI, VADODARA)

The day I finally received permission to conduct the tests, after a great struggle from the Public School Board in Vadodara, I ran into a group of children playing very cheerfully in front of the flat where I was staying. The two children whose parents lived next door told me that the girls they were playing with did not go to their school. Beaming with a sense of pride, they clarified that they attended a private English-medium school, while their playmates attended a public school in the neighborhood. I saw the beautiful face of serendipity in the situation and the next morning walked over to the public school, which was exclusively for girls. The parents of these girls lived in the area. Most of them worked as maids and gardeners for the upper-class residences and lived in their own arrangements. Some parents lived in the ghetto area nearby.

These children from the scheduled groups did not have to face the poor environmental conditions. Compared to their counterparts who lived in the isolated ghettoes, girls from these groups had other advantages. They played with the privileged children and, to some extent, participated in mainstream Hindu cultural activities. They were highly motivated and talked about their future lives with a sense of ambition that was conspicuously absent in the children who grew up in the ghettoes. The parents of these girls also supported them and let them dream about a better life.

The principal and teachers were also distinctly different. Most of these teachers came from the scheduled groups and understood the value of education. They were all enthusiastic and competent. The principal as well as the teachers talked frankly about the fumbling educational system and the obstacles that they encountered regularly. It seemed that the difficulties they faced made them more resourceful and adventurous. The situation in the other two public schools where I saw the teachers interact with their pupils from scheduled groups was in sharp contrast: the children from scheduled groups were treated with obvious disdain; the teachers assumed that they were to be promoted to higher grades without learning anything.

SUBJECTS

After talking with the school principal and the teacher in charge of grade three, I decided to test all the 47 girls in this grade. Their ages ranged between seven and 11 years. Only one child was 11 years old, and five of the girls did not know their ages. While six of the girls were seven years old, 11, 13, and 17 girls were eight, nine, and 10, respectively. They all enjoyed good general health and did not have any problem related to vision and hearing. No child suffered from an overt mental or physical developmental handicap.

Eighteen of the 47 subjects in this advantaged scheduled group expressed a definite direction in career goals. Six of them declared that they would become doctors and two more added that they would like to be child specialists; one preferred nursing. Four students suggested that they would become "madams", that is, teachers. While two girls expressed a clear preference for the life of a housewife, one said that she would definitely become a political leader and devote her life to national service like Bapu, that is, the Father of the Nation, Mohandas Karamchand Gandhi. One indicated a preference for a private business, specifically running a sewing class. They were all deeply aware of the hard life their parents had to experience and they helped their siblings and mothers after school hours. I am sure that these children have developed a sense of what Subramanian (1991) calls "conscient-isation of the community" which he defines as "... awakening of consciousness, a change of outlook, an increased, accurate and realistic awareness of society ..." (p. 21).

All the parents of these advantaged children from scheduled groups spoke the standard dialect of Gujarati. These children used Sanskrit words more often than their upper-class playmates, most of whom, attended English-medium private schools and used a lot of English. Most of the children from scheduled groups wore designer clothes, which were hand-downs from their parents' upper-class employers. Compared to the disadvantaged children from scheduled groups, these children in the advantaged group also get better nutrition; they get some food from the upper-class neighbors. The presence of the expensive houses in an upper-class area with big incomes, flashy cars, and conversations about foreign travel are motivating factors for these children.

TESTS

1. **Picture Naming:** Ten familiar items from each of the four categories of objects, birds, fruits, and flowers were selected. The pictures of these items were pasted onto cards. The pictures were cut out from popular posters, which are sold in the educational tool market.
2. **Symbol Recognition:** Fifteen hand-drawn designs of nonsense objects were painted on cards. Each card contained three symbols, one of which was the target. Children were shown a symbol on a card and asked to examine the card in front of them. The task was to say "yes" or "no" to the question: "Is this picture on this card? Show it to me." Essentially, the task required visual target search and matching.
3. **Objects in Spatial Relations (On/Under/Left/Right/):** This test was a modification of the experimental task designed by Landau (1993). Nonsense objects were hand-drawn and given nonsense names, which were totally unfamiliar to the local children. These pictures were placed on/under/to the left of/ to the right of a hand-drawn table. The instruction was as follows: "Look, this is Lordes. Tell me if Lordes is under the table in this picture. Just say yes or no."
4. **Oral Repetition of Words:** Thirty familiar regular words consisting of three, four, and five akṣərəs (10 in each of the three categories) were selected. Thirty nonsense word-like akṣərə strings following the same pattern were created.
5. **Rhyming: Odd Word Out:** The children were presented with groups of three words, two of which rhymed (for a total of 15 items). The task was to pick out the odd word.
6. **Identification of Phonemes in akṣərəs:** The children were shown cards (15 in total) with written akṣərəs and were asked if a given vowel or consonant was in the akṣərə on the card on the table. The vowel or consonant in question was given in its

spoken form. The instruction was: "Is there /u/ in this *akṣarə* /pu/?" All 15 items were basic *akṣarəs*.

7. **Visual *akṣarə* Matching:** This task was similar to symbol matching (Block A-2). The cards (15 in total) contained *akṣarəs* instead of nonverbal meaningless symbols. Each card contained three written *akṣarəs* with visual similarity.

8. **Spoken–Written *akṣarə* Matching:** This task was similar to the visual *akṣarə* matching. The subject heard a spoken *akṣarə* and was asked to point to its written form. Each card consisted of a consonant with all the vowels: *ka, ki, ko, kau, ku*, etc., (15 in total).

9. **Visual Word Matching:** In this test, words replaced *akṣarəs* (15 in total).

10. **Spoken–Written Word Matching:** The subject heard a spoken word and was asked to point to its written form on the card. Each card consisted of three written words (15 cards in total).

11. **Picture–Written Word Matching:** The subject was shown a familiar picture and was asked to point to a corresponding written word. Each card consisted of three written words (15 cards).

12. **Paragraph Comprehension:** A short paragraph (six lines) was selected from a grade three textbook story about a crow. The subject was asked to read the paragraph on the card and answer five questions about the story. The five questions were factual and required no inferential processing.

13. **Oral Reading of Regular and Nonsense Words with cv, cvc, and vc Syllables:** Each category consisted of 10 words. The words were composed of two cv, cvc, and vc syllables. The question of interest was whether the *akṣarəs* standing for c, the coda in cvc would be read as c or cv. For example, would /yog/ be read as /yog/ (cv c) or /yoga/ (cv cv)?

PROCEDURE

The school principal graciously arranged for me to have some room and two chairs every morning. Subjects were tested individually. At each session, subjects were given only half of the test battery. This practice was maintained to make sure that the children would not be tired during, or at the end of the session. This also helped me to keep my promise that my work with the pupils would not disturb their regular classroom learning.

Practice was provided for each test. It was not difficult to see whether the task was easy or out of reach for the subjects. All the subjects, including those whose performance was poor, liked being tested.

The testing was conducted in a supposedly quiet environment. However, the word "quiet" must be understood in the context of the public schools in India. In my perception, these children and teachers functioned despite all the clutter around them. They complained about the furniture and other things but never about the noisy background. It looked like they needed the noise to go about naturally in their world.

Major Trends in Results

All the 47 third graders did extremely well in naming, comprehension of spatial relations in language use, oral repetition of words, and non-verbal symbol recognition. Unlike their disadvantaged counterparts from the scheduled groups, their naming responses involved only standard vocabulary. This may be taken as an indication of adequate general cognitive–linguistic development.

How about the tests which required rhyme detection and identification of consonant and vowel phonemes in akṣaras, that is, akṣara segmentation? Both the children from the mainstream and the disadvantaged scheduled groups found these tests beyond their reach. The girls from these groups who played with the mainstream children and lived in and around upper-class residences, like their mainstream counterparts, could not detect rhyme and segment akṣaras.

The advantaged girls from scheduled groups were not a homogeneous group in their performance in akṣara and word matching. Out of the 47, 14 subjects behaved like their counterparts in the disadvantaged outlier group. These 14 subjects showed some positive signs in visual akṣara and word matching and their responses in picture-written word matching were not entirely random. However, when they were asked to match spoken words with their written representations, they were almost random in their responses.

The remaining 33 subjects exhibited an amazingly high level of performance in akṣara and word matching. The task of matching spoken akṣaras and words with written akṣaras and words did not baffle them. Whenever the responses were not correct, it seemed that it was something other than the ability related to lexical processing that blocked them. They seemed to know the words and could retrieve them with ease.

The trend of positive signs in visual lexical processing in 16 out of the 33 subjects is also seen clearly in the test for paragraph comprehension. Even though these 16 subjects were poor in *akṣara* segmentation and rhyming, they read the paragraph fluently, with appropriate pauses, and answered the five comprehension questions correctly. Thirteen subjects showed a reasonable level of comprehension, but their oral reading was poor. They read the paragraph *akṣara* by *akṣara* without indicating any sign of lexicality or wordness and sentences. It seems that these advantaged third graders from scheduled groups can process the written form of language for comprehension without the skills involved in fluent oral reading. The disassociation between comprehension and oral reading processes was clearly observable in one subject who read the paragraph fluently but could not answer any of the five comprehension questions. The 14 subjects referred to earlier in relation to their poor performance in spoken–written *akṣara* and word matching looked at paragraph reading as an entirely strange and baffling task.

Turning now to the test which required oral reading of regular and nonsense words composed of cv, cvc, and vc syllables, let us first see how the subjects handled the *akṣara*s representing pure consonants, that is, without the vowel schwa. Remarkably, only those with top performance in all other tests read words with cvc and vc syllables correctly, that is, read cvc as cv and c and vc as v and c as independent *akṣara*s. The majority of the 47 subjects read cvc words as cvcv and vc words as vcv, that is, they did not recognize pure consonants in the coda position as *akṣara*s; they added the vowel schwa. Those who correctly read cvc and vc also performed well in matching written words with their corresponding spoken words and pictures. What is significant about the ability to read words with cvc and vc syllables correctly is that it may be related to the development of the sense of lexicality or wordness. Equally interesting theoretically is that the ability to read cvc and vc words correctly is not related to superior performance in *akṣara* segmentation, that is, the ability to identify consonant and vowel phonemes.

Is the ability to read cvc and vc words correctly developmental? To answer this question in a preliminary way, I tested six girls from the grade four class. Out of these six subjects, five of them demonstrated perfect performance in recognizing pure consonant *akṣaras*, that is, they read cvc and vc syllables in words correctly without any hesitation. Subject six did badly in all oral word reading categories, including words with all cv syllables. These children from the advantaged scheduled group in grade five ignored the vowel signs and showed no signs indicating a sense of wordness or lexicality just like the children from the disadvantaged group did.

In overview, how do the girls in the advantaged scheduled group attending a public school measure up when compared to their disadvantaged sisters and brothers and the mainstream private school children? Out of the 47 girls in the advantaged scheduled group from a public school, 16 can clearly match the mainstream private school children in all the tests developed to gauge the processes and skills involved in early reading. In the disadvantaged group, this was true in the case of only one child, who was indeed an exceptional eight-year-old for any group, let alone the disadvantaged outlier children.

There were three outstanding trends uncovered in the test performance of the advantaged scheduled group. First, all the children showed signs of adequate general cognitive–linguistic development. Their test scores in naming, nonverbal symbol recognition, spatial relations in language use, and oral repetition of complex words were strikingly good. Second, all the children were conspicuously poor in identifying consonants and vowels in *akṣaras*.

Third, almost 30 percent of the girls in the advantaged scheduled group showed clear signs of success in recognizing the orthographic form of words and their picture associations. These positive signs were also apparent in paragraph comprehension. This association between written word recognition and paragraph comprehension was noticeable in the absence of the ability to match spoken and written words and in the absence to recognize the component parts of *akṣaras*.

The problem of splitting the cvc and vc syllables into cv + c and v + c for *akṣara* formation is not common in all Indian languages. In Kannada, a Dravidian language, and Oriya, an Indo-Aryan language, for example, there are no c *akṣaras*. The name *Ajit* in Oriya is usually pronounced *Ajita* and the name *Shankar* is pronounced *Shankara* in Kannada. However, there are ongoing sociolinguistic changes in Orissa and Karnataka. The schwa at the end of words, as in *Ajita* and *Shankara*, is disappearing. There are linguistically fascinating historical changes taking place in the different Indo-Aryan and Dravidian languages at the moment in India.

Chapter Eleven

CHILDREN FROM SCHEDULED GROUPS: POOR READERS OR DYSLEXICS?

INTRODUCTION

Gujarati-speaking children from the mainstream groups attending private schools in Vadodara seem to experience no serious difficulties in learning to read. On the other hand, as far as the children from scheduled groups attending public schools is concerned, a sizeable number of them, coming from both the disadvantaged and advantaged groups, face nontrivial problems in some reading acquisition mechanisms. The issue of an appropriate label for the reading problems observed in such children, some of which appear to be dyslexia-type, involves some questions with interesting methodological and theoretical consequences. The possibility of dyslexia in children raised in risky environmental conditions, especially in the context of the culture of poverty and the low caste status in India, is a centrally important question. Eisenberg (1978) and Fletcher et al., (1999), among others, have raised the question of dyslexia in disadvantaged children. But the concept of "specificity" and the associated methodological constraints related to subject selection are still dominant.

There are several labels associated with children's problems in learning to read. Researchers and practitioners in different domains use terms like "poor readers," "backward readers," "disabled readers," and "dyslexics." Shaywitz et al., (1992) look at failure in reading acquisition only statistically and consider it as the lower end of the normal distribution of scores on achievement in learning to read. However, they admit that some children "may, in fact, have a reading disability of qualitatively different origin or a unique biologic defect" (p. 149). Some researchers just use the term "disabled readers" and examine performance in selected processes, for example, phonological awareness and naming speed. The term "developmental dyslexia" is conceptualized in relation to specific cellular abnormalities in cortical areas, visual–auditory pathways, corpus callosum, cerebellum, and reading-specific defective genes on chromosomes 6 and 15. In developmental neuropsychology and psychiatry, the term "development dyslexia" is defined in terms of "specificity," that is, failure in reading acquisition without deficits in general cognitive–linguistic development in children who also do not suffer from what Rutter and Madge (1976) call "cycles of disadvantage." In operational terms, children with inadequate schooling opportunities and poor parents are not included in studies on "specific reading retardation," "specific reading disability," or "developmental dyslexia." This methodological strategy, which was devised for subject selection to tease apart specifically dylexia-related deficits, entered the practice of clinical diagnosis in the disciplines dealing with learning disabilities. Hence, children reared in poverty and its associated environmental conditions are not seriously considered when compensatory special education services are conceptualized, planned, and delivered.

This exclusionary framework is gradually eroding. The role of IQ in dyslexia diagnosis is now considered irrelevant (Siegel, 1988; Stanovich, 1991). Siegel (1988) reports that there are significant differences between "the reading disabled" and normally achieving children at each IQ level, but no significant differences among reading-disabled children at each IQ level. Stanovich (1986) has considered the problem of Mathew effects in this context. Mathew effects are important so far as the role of reading in the development of IQ and other related cognitive abilities is concerned. While the children who read well go ahead in other cognitive abilities, those with poor reading skills are left behind, in reading as well as in other related domains.

The other exclusionary criteria associated with poverty and poor schooling conditions have also been found questionable. Eisenberg (1978) considers the exclusionary criteria for the diagnosis of "reading failure" and highlights the lack of reliable criteria "to distinguish the lower-class dyslexic from the one who is a backward reader for other reasons." He refers to his research on poverty, social depreciation, and child development and points out that "private school reading scores far exceed those for public schools" (p. 37). Eisenberg (*ibid.*, p. 36) exposes the myth of "the middle-class dyslexic child" by pointing out a direct correlation between achievement in learning to read and social class, as reported by large-scale community-wide surveys. He argues "… reading failure is the final common expression for more than one and probably multiple underlying causal factors" (p. 33). In their comprehensive and penetrating analysis of the con-ceptual and methodological issues in research on dyslexia, Fletcher et al., (1999, pp. 276–77) point out that:

> Much of the research on dyslexia has explored the relationship of cognitive and biological factors, but the contribution of social and environmental factors should not be discounted. A particu-larly difficult problem is the possibility, largely unexamined, that the phenotype associated with reading disability may not vary across potential causes. Hence, even in poor readers with a history of social deprivation, the initial problems reflect difficulties in learning decoding skills, and the cognitive correlates are similar to those in children who read poorly with no history of social deprivation.

Both for subject selection in research studies and diagnosis for treat-ment or admission to special education classes, only "children with average levels of potential ability, poor reading skills, and the absence of problems due to cultural factors, instructional methods, and sensory or acquired neurological deficits" (Fletcher et al., 1989, p. 334) get attention.

The dyslexic neurobiological abnormalities include lesions and cellular differences in specific cortical areas in both the hemispheres, the magnocellular channel in the visual as well as the auditory pathways passing through the thalamus onto the cortex, the corpus callosum, the cerebellum, and so on. These cellular abnormalities may "implicate a developmental window beginning early during the second half of pregnancy and terminating by the end of the second year of postnatal life" (Rosen, 1998, p. 57). The cortical networks are in charge of higher mental functions, which include, for example, representation and processing for language, thinking, and attention. The visual and auditory pathways transmit the information picked up by the eyes and ears, respectively, to the cortical networks. The corpus callosum is a commissure, which serves as an information transmission pathway between the two cortical surfaces. The thalamus is a central junctional station through which information from different modalities passes up and down. The cerebellum plans and executes specific types of movement and also plays a role in cognitive–linguistic functioning. Cellular aberrations were observed in postmortem dissections in a small number of dyslexic subjects as well as through *in vivo* neuroimaging technology. Before looking at the loci of the abnormalities, here follows a succinct overview of the relevant brain structures and pathways.

In the architectural design of brain structures involved in language processing, there seems to be no doubt that the perisylvian region is implicated in dyslexic development (Filipek et al., 1999). This abnormal migration of cells in cortical genesis may be related to a structural change in the planum temporale which is "not a distinct structure, but rather is a triangular landmark located on the superior surface of the temporal lobe just prior to Heschl's gyrus" (*ibid.*, p. 4). The planum temporale is a subregion located in the Sylvian fissure; it is close to the primary auditory cortex (Heschl's gyrus) and includes a part of Wernicke's Area associated with sound patterns for words and listening comprehension (Shapleske et al., 1999). In most right-handed people, the planum temporale is larger in the left hemisphere than in the right hemisphere. This asymmetry is absent in the dissected dyslexic brains (see Rosen, 1998 for a discussion). It may be that these cellular abnormalities are related to the core dyslexic deficit, namely, lack of phonological awareness, and hence, the inability to read nonsense words.

Cellular pathology has also been observed in the magnocellular-transient channel in both the visual and the auditory pathways from the eyes and ears to the cortex. Postmortem dissections show abnormal cellular characteristics in two thalamic structures, namely, the visual lateral geniculate nucleus and the auditory medial geniculate nucleus in the magnocellular channel. The impaired functioning of the transient-magno channel has also been corroborated by research in psychophysics, physiology, and neuro-imaging (Breitmeyer, 1989; Eden et al., 1995; Livingstone et al., 1991; Lovegrove et al., 1986; Slaghui et al., 1993; Stein and Walsh, 1997). Filipek et al., (1999) cite the func-tional magnetic resonance imaging (fMRI) studies by Demb et al., (1998), which showed that the presentation of moving stimuli failed to activate the magnocellular visual system in their dyslexic sample appropriately.

In addition to the cellular abnormalities in the perisylvian cortical region and the magnocellular-transient channel in both the visual and auditory pathways, dyslexic pathology is reported to have deviance in the morphology of the corpus callosum and the cerebellum. Larsen et al., (1992), Hynd et al., (1995), and Rumsey et al., (1996) report dyslexia-related abnormalities in the corpus callosum, which lead to disturbance in interhemispheric information transmission. Nicolson and Fawcett (1999) have recently reported aberrations in the cerebellum of the dyslexic children in their study. The role of the cerebellum in some cognitive abilities is now recognized (Leiner et al., 1993; Schmahmann, 1996).

Can the neurobiological abnormalities observed in association with clinically defined dyslexia account for some of the core psycholinguistic and other deficits? It must be noted that dyslexia is diagnosed in different ways and the different studies involve different subject samples in different sizes, using different stimuli, and with different tasks. It is difficult to talk about generalizable patterns of dyslexic performance in terms of the statistical difficulties and the problems involved in experimental control (Coleman, 1981; Rubin, 1989). There are also other methodological and conceptual issues specific to the domain of dyslexia research (Fletcher et al., 1999). However, taken together, the cumulative research suggests some core deficits and interpretations, which can be considered as a working file for suggestive clues about dyslexic performance and the associated neurobiological abnormalities.

In language processing, dyslexic deficits are mainly at or below the level of the word; the level of performance in other domains of language, in general, is within the range of the lower end of normal distribution (Doehring et al., 1981). The reported deficits at the syntactic–semantic level might be the consequences of dyslexic experience (Patel, 1983). At the sublexical level, dyslexic children find it difficult to perceive and manipulate the sound units that make up words (Doehring et al., 1981; Rack et al., 1992; Stanovich, 1988). At the lexical level, dyslexic children are slow in retrieving words from the mental dictionary (Bowers and Swanson, 1991; Wolf and Obregon, 1992).

At the level of brain architecture and language processing, both the difficulties related to phonological awareness and naming can be explained in terms of the many cellular malformations in the perisylvian region. It must be noted that the abnormalities are both in the visual and the auditory pathways as well as in the perisylvian region. To the extent that temporal processing is involved in the phonological awareness and naming tasks, these deficits can also be accounted for in relation to the magnocellular abnormalities in the medial geniculate nucleus, which is an auditory way station in the thalamus. As it is in the case of the visual system, the auditory pathway between the inner ear and the auditory cortex consists of two parallel channels: nucleus magnocellularis and nucleus angularis. The nucleus magnocellularis carries only frequency-specific information in speech patterns, while the nucleus angularis is responsible for the transmission of intensity-specific speech information (Konishi, 1995). The defect in the fast magno-transient transmission channel may account for the inability of dyslexic children to process the rapid and high contrast visual and auditory information (Eden et al., 1995; Tallal et al., 1993). Chase (1996) points out that the magnocellular-transient system provides information, in the form of low spatial frequency components, which facilitates learning to read. Chase also makes an interesting suggestion that slow processing of low spatial frequency components by dyslexics can "impair the development of lexical memory and slow lexical access" (*ibid.*, p. 144).

In a functional magnetic resonance imaging (fMRI) study attempting to neurally trace the inability to read phonologically legal nonsense words, Shaywitz et al., (1998) observed significant differences in brain activation patterns in dyslexics in tasks that make progressive demands on phonological analysis. The study demonstrates a link between the cognitive/behavioral deficit characterizing dyslexic readers and anomalous activation patterns in both posterior and anterior brain regions:

> Thus, within a large posterior cortical system including Wernicke's area, the angular gyrus, the extrastriate and striate cortex, dyslexic readers fail to systematically increase activation as the difficulty of mapping print onto phonologic structures increases. In contrast, in anterior regions including the inferior frontal gyrus, and Broadmann's areas 46, 47, 11 dyslexic readers show a pattern of overactivation in response to even the simplest phonologic task (*ibid.*, p. 2638).

In a positron emission tomography (PET) study involving dyslexic men, Horwitz et al., (1998) focus on the functional connectivity of the angular gyrus, which is implicated in Shaywitz et al., (1998). Horwitz et al., (1998) also relate the dysfunction in the angular gyrus to the magnocellular system:

> The loss of functional connectivity in dyslexia between the left angular gyrus and the occipitotemporal region containing V5/MT is interesting in that several reports have suggested a fundamental abnormality in the magnocellular system, of which V5/MT is a part in developmental dyslexia.

The middle temporal area or MT which is located in the posterior superior temporal sulcus, is a part of the extrastriate visual processing network: It is one of the major recipient areas of the magnocellular channel which passes through the lower parietal lobe and projects to the frontal eye fields (Breitmeyer, 1989, p. 538).

Whether the pathogenesis of dyslexia in children is caused by the defective genetic markers on chromosomes 6 and 15 (Grigorenko et al., 1997) or some environmental toxins and social depreciation, or by interactive mechanisms, is an important research question, especially in the context of children from scheduled groups.

READING PROBLEMS IN CHILDREN FROM SCHEDULED GROUPS

How do the problems experienced by the children from scheduled groups in India compare with the situation of "the poor children" in the United States studied by Chall et al., (1990)? What is labelled "poverty" in the two countries is radically different, quantitatively as well as qualitatively. However, it may be that the observed similarities and differences may throw some light on the association between reading acquisition and "cycles of disadvantage." I will pay attention only to indicative trends rather than to detailed analyses.

The low-income children in grades two and six in Chall et al.'s study generally achieved at their expected grade levels. But, the grade six children were found to be about half a year below grade norms. Both above-average and below-average children performed relatively well in reading paragraphs for comprehension. However, both word recognition in isolation and decoding presented problems. The difficulty in isolated word recognition and decoding perhaps was less of a problem in the higher grades. After grade four, these children from low-income areas performed poorly on word meaning and comprehension; they also found it difficult to acquire academic vocabulary. What is relevant in the context of the children from scheduled groups is that, for the American low-income children, "achievement in beginning reading is *more highly associated with word recognition and decoding than with language and cognition*" (*ibid.*, p. 109, italics added).

It is necessary to remember that the low-income children in Chall et al.'s study were selected to represent "a wide range of reading achievement" and "those who were at the extreme ends of the distribution" were excluded from the study. Also not included in the study of the low-income children were those "who were learning-disabled, dyslexic, or language-impaired and whose low literacy and language development might well have a neurological basis" (*ibid.*, p. 17).

The children from scheduled groups were not selected on the basis of any criterion; they represented the children whose parents belonged to the Scheduled Castes and Scheduled Tribes. They lived either in isolated ghettoes on the outskirts of mainstream residential areas or in the compounds of the upper-class houses and attended public schools. Under these circumstances, children with very low intelligence bordering on mental retardation or specific language impairment, however, are not likely to be in school. However, the Indian scheduled group tested here is bound to include the learning-disabled, in general, and the dyslexic, in particular, as they appear to be normal, and perhaps, above-average in nonverbal intelligence.

The children from scheduled groups, in the disadvantaged as well as the advantaged groups, are like their counterparts from mainstream groups in private schools; that is, they are generally not backward or deviant in general linguistic–cognitive development. Their vocabulary is clearly within the normal range observed in children from mainstream groups in private schools. They can repeat complex words with clear standard articulation. This trend matches the results of the Chall et al.'s study of the poor areas around Boston. For the reader who is interested in exclusionary criteria, American low income and the Indian scheduled children meet the requirement regarding normal general cognitive–linguistic development.

What might suggest an important insight is the ceiling-level performance of children from scheduled groups in the test which involves spatial relations: Where is Lordes? (on/under/to the left of/to the right of the table?). This test is a modification of a section of Barbara Landau's (1993) "where's what and what's where" test which requires the comprehension of spatial language and spatial cognition. In a landmark paper, Landau and Jackendoff (1994) link the magnocellular-parvocellular information transmission neural pathways with the where and what cognitive–linguistic representation–processing systems. Recall the earlier account of the distinct functions of the magno-parvo channels in visual processing. Landau and Jackendoff look at the two functionally and cellularly distinct systems of visual information processing channels and treat the "what" and "where" systems as cognitive–semantic universals and consider the way they are acquired in psycholinguistic development.

Landau's (1993, p. 277) research suggests that these distinct representations of "where" and "what" neural–cognitive–linguistic systems are reflected in children's early comprehension, production, and learning of names for objects and places:

> By the age of two and a half, children have a respectable stock of spatial prepositions and by age four, they have even learned some of the most complex English prepositions, such as in front of and behind.

This developmental pattern showing the separation of the "where" and "what" systems has been documented cross-linguistically and in deaf children.

Can we locate any specific cortical mechanism associated with language processing? That the outlier children perform at the ceiling-level in a task which makes them use their "where" and "what" systems indicates that their magnocellular and the parvocellular pathways in the visual system may be, in general, intact. It remains to be seen if the magno–parvo channels in some children from scheduled groups are impaired in some specific way related to reading acquisition processes. The adjoining cortical areas in the parietal and the temporal lobes must also be functioning adequately in some way: Many of them can match written *akṣaras* and words. Since most of these outlier children cannot match spoken *akṣaras* and words with their written forms, it is the auditory temporal areas involving the planum temporale that might be less than adequate in functioning in these scheduled children. Recall that the same children perform badly on oral word reading, *akṣara* segmentation, and rhyming. Given the environmentally explosive conditions in the way these children are conceived and raised, it is likely that the nucleus magnocellularis in the auditory pathway get adversely affected.

Can we, then, formulate a research hypothesis that a significant number of such children from scheduled groups, more often from the disadvantaged group, might be handicapped in terms of compromised auditory processing mechanisms specifically linked to reading acquisition processes? It seems that children who are successful in learning to read form both the auditory and the orthographic lexical–semantic subsystems with their interlinking networks by grade four. The compromised auditory–orthographic–semantic interlinking connections in these children, especially in the disadvantaged group, might block some specific processes in reading acquisition. Whatever mechanisms help them to match written *akṣaras* and words, perhaps, develop without making a link with the spoken lexical storage. Hence, in oral reading, they recognize mostly consonants and pronounce them in isolation without being able to retrieve words from the mental dictionary guided by these consonant skeletons.

The question of the difficulty experienced by children failing in reading acquisition in dealing with vowels needs to be investigated within the framework of auditory neurophysiology. The special difficulty in vowel recognition in oral reading by the majority of the disadvantaged children from scheduled groups and the minority of the advantaged children from the same groups may indicate a deficit at some subcortical level. It is not unreasonable to suggest that the terribly toxic environment, third-world poverty, the viscid sense of shame associated with the low caste status can cause cellular abnormalities in both the visual and the auditory systems at the subcortical level, especially in the lateral geniculate and the medial geniculate nuclei in the thalamus. As noted earlier, vowels are processed subcortically without any significant input from the primary auditory cortex. These children are relatively less poor in recognizing consonants in oral reading, which may imply that they have no problem in the auditory primary cortex. The left hemisphere seems to be endowed with a processing mechanism, which deals with the transitions in the consonantal spectra. Phillips et al., (1991) point out that steady-state and transient sounds may be processed at different levels: Auditory cortical neurons have no temporal representation of the fine time structure of vowels. Research indicates that vowel discrimination survives bilateral lesions of the auditory cortex in humans. For them "The discrimination of sounds whose identities reside in their fine periodic time structure may rely more on brainstem processing in which the temporal structure of the sounds is better represented" (*ibid.*, p. 353). Perhaps the defective mechanisms are located in the subcortical route.

The debate on the value of phonological representations in reading acquisition in its current state is simply superficial. For example, it ignores the specific role phonological information plays in linking information from word to word in saccadic eye movements. Research suggests that phonological codes are used in integrating information across saccades in word identification and reading (Pollastek et al., 1992). Earlier, I have indicated, in relation to the children from the disadvantaged, scheduled groups, that the developmental course of their mental dictionaries appeared to be different. The processes and mechanisms involved in the emergence and development of written language representation and processing must have some specific internal as well as external requirements.

Whether dyslexia-type neural inadequacy can be caused by environmental toxins and social depreciation, in general, and specifically, in association with the culture of poverty and the caste system in India, is a question of critical importance. The cultural–social–linguistic input available to the children from the mainstream groups is conspicuously absent at home as well as in the communities where most of the parents from the disadvantaged scheduled groups live. Adding to this are the horrendous environmental conditions to which these children are exposed from the day they are conceived. Most of the mothers from such groups suffer from both negative stress in daily life and the ever present pernicious effects of hundreds of toxins which envelop their dwellings. These effects are exacerbated during India's monsoons and hot summer, which, together, persist for eight months in a year.

The statistical association between reading problems, on the one hand, and geographical location (inner-city ghettoes), large family size, low socioeconomic status, late birth position in the family, and male sex, on the other, is robust (Eisenberg, 1978; Rutter, 1978). The epidemiological study of "reading disability" by Badian (1984) points to some environmental correlates, specifically, hot summer temperatures in the perinatal period.

Of course, it might be that some of these children might have defective genes in chromosomes 15 and 6, as is the case of American children. Grigorenko et al., (1997) suggest two genotypic-phenotypic links: Phonological awareness on chromosome 6 and single word reading on chromosome 15. Current research on the genetics of dyslexia indicates that heritability in the ability for word recognition is not specific to phonological coding. Olson et al., (1989) examined the separate contributions of phonological coding and orthographic coding skills in dyslexic subjects to genetic and environmental variance in word recognition. A recent reanalysis of the data suggests that the heritable variance in word recognition might be associated with phonological as well as orthographic coding (Olson, 2001). Olson et al., (1989) cite Gough et al., (1992) whose research points to the primary role of experience in the environment in learning to read specific words, especially in "the development of word-level orthographic codes" (p. 345). Can we apply Olson et al.'s results and interpretation to the children from scheduled groups who show some ability to match written akṣaras and words and fare badly in spoken-written akṣara and word matching, oral word reading, akṣara segmentation, and rhyming?

In such children, especially those who grow up in developmentally risky environmental conditions, "Teratological events and abnormal genetic events may be expressed through similar mechanisms of abnormal development" (Adams, 1999, p. 463). Animal models of developmental dyslexia suggest that events occurring early in corticogenesis may lead to developmental neuropathologic lesions (Rosen, 1998). It is reasonable to assume that a sizeable number of the children from scheduled groups would be diagnosed as dyslexic by clinicians if they were presented as otherwise normal children.

What is likely to be critically influential is the way the auditory and the visual systems progress through the various subcortical stations toward their developmental pathways leading to the primary and secondary auditory and visual cortical areas. In the case of the auditory system, "the processing of intensity and and frequency information appears to reach similar to naïve adults by 6 months of age." Interestingly, in the context of dyslexia, however, "temporal processing appears to have a more protracted development continuing at least into the preschool years" (Aslin and Hunt, 2001, p. 208). To the extent that magnocellular abnormality is involved in the emergence of dyslexic performance, the developmental course of the magno and parvo pathways is relevant. In adults, the two pathways are considered to be "quasi-independent," but "when they first emerge there may be considerable overlap in how they process visual information" (Dannemiller, 2001, p. 231).

Recent research suggests that the presence of a magnocellular defect depends on the subtype of dyslexia in question (Borsting et al., 1996). The literature on subtypes in learning disabilities, in general, and developmental reading disabilities, in particular, makes no reference to social deprivation and poverty (Rourke, 1985). As Fletcher and Satz (1985) suggest, each subtype shows a different pattern of development. What sort of subtypes will emerge and change developmentally in the Indian children from scheduled groups with the varying degrees and types of "cycles of disadvantage" is a question that is likely to advance theory, methodology, and remediation related to learning disabilities.

Chapter Twelve

CONCLUSION

What are the trends and insights emerging out of my exploratory research on reading acquisition in Gujarati-speaking children in India, which can impact the current models of reading acquisition and developmental dyslexia?

This volume can be divided into three parts. The first part provides a scholarly background on the ancient Vedic tradition of oral learning and its links, first with the rise of phonetics, and second, with the analysis of the Brāhmī orthographic unit, *akṣara*, in terms of syllable quantity and *matra* values. The second part shows how the culture of oral learning and recitation fosters phonological awareness of the *akṣara* as reading emerges in language development. For a link between this background and the empirical studies, I have sketched a cognitive–linguistic–neural processing system for reading. The studies involve mainstream children who attend private schools and children from scheduled groups who attend public schools. The latter are divided into two groups. The first group, referred to here as "disadvantaged," included children (boys and girls) whose parents lived in isolated areas at the outskirts of mainstream residential areas. The second group, referred to here as "advantaged," consisted of only girls whose parents lived in upper-class residential compounds.

Considering the performance of the majority of these children from scheduled groups in specific tests related to reading, I have raised the issue of the diagnostic label for these children; that is, whether these children should be considered dyslexic.

I have tried to show that the *akṣara* is a subsyllabic unit, which can be accounted for in terms of syllable quantity or some current models of syllable structure. In the Indian phonetic framework, it can be explained with reference to *matra* values: The *akṣara* can bear one or two *matra*s, as in /ma/ and /drau/. The *akṣara*s consist of phonemes, but they are whole units, phonologically as well as in terms topographical design, that is, the visuospatial script relations. In writing, words are sequences of *akṣara*s, not of phonemes. The ancient Indian phoneticians distinguished between "syllable quantity" and "vowel length." The concept of *matra*, which represents the primary measure of syllable quantity, corresponds to the modern linguistic term "mora." The *akṣara* stands for v, vv, c, cc, ccv, cccv, ccvv, cccvv. In traditional terms, the *akṣara* corresponds to a short or long vowel or a diphthong with or without a preceding consonant or a consonant cluster. The *akṣara*s carrying the nasal dot called *anusvara* may appear to be an exception to this general rule in most of the Brāhmī scripts used in India. However, the ancient phoneticians recognized the consonantal as well as the vocalic features of *anusvara*. Hence, the *akṣara* with an *anusvara* can be treated as cvv or vv. In orthographic form, the *akṣara*s are demarcated; that is, the reader can clearly see the visuospatial configuration of the *akṣara* in words. The phonetic–phonological principles underlying the different Brāhmī scripts used now in India, Tibet, Thailand, Myanmar, and Kampuchia, among others, need to be investigated within a framework integrating the ancient Indian language science and the current experimentally–theoretically motivated models of syllable organization.

The spoken correlate of the *akṣara* is available to the mainstream Hindu children in cultural ecology which is dominated by the ancient Vedic tradition of oral learning and recitation. The timing unit in oral learning and recitation is the *akṣara*. Children experience a great of oral learning and recitation which fosters their awareness about the *akṣara* unit which in turn governs the pattern of accentuation in Vedic recitation.

For the Gujarati-speaking children in India, the *akṣara* is a primary unit in beginning reading acquisition. The mainstream children attending Gujarati-medium private schools can read words and paragraphs for both oral transmission and comprehension. What is interesting is that they perform poorly on tests which require word segmentation below the level of the akṣarə. It is only after grade four that they can segment akṣarəs into their phonemic components. Until then, they progress in reading acquisition and reach the levels expected by their teachers and parents.

It seems that akṣarə awareness in mainstream children is fostered by cultural ecology, mainly the Vedic oral tradition, which is not available to those children whose parents are from scheduled groups. The majority of the children from scheduled groups, especially those who face environmental toxins and social depreciation, are blocked in reading acquisition at the initial stage. They recognize some consonants in akṣarəs and simply cannot reach the level of word recognition. At times they can match written akṣarəs and words, but they cannot match spoken akṣarəs and words with their written counterparts. Otherwise, they seem to be normal in general cognitive–linguistic development. The picture is a lot better in the case of those children from scheduled groups, who grow up in the upper-class compounds and play with the children from the mainstream. Most of these female pupils perform like their mainstream counterparts in private schools. The number of the children with reading problems in this advantaged group is significantly smaller, but the deficits in learning to read appear to be the same.

I have speculated that the locus of the failure in reading acquisition among children from scheduled groups may be the organization of the mental dictionary. It seems that, whatever the neurobiological bottleneck in reading acquisition in these children, it definitely disrupts the development of the phonological–orthographic–semantic representations and their interlinking networks in the mental lexicon. And this problem may be related to the development of the auditory processing system in these children. This may be, in part, a consequence of the lack of the beneficial ecological input routinely available to the children from the mainstream. It may also be the effect of the environmental toxins that surround their dwellings, the nutritionally deficient food, and the social depreciation associated with the Hindu caste system. Whether this damage can cause dyslexic-type genetic and/or neurobiological aberrations is a critical research question.

The pattern of results shows that children speaking Gujarati, an Indo-Aryan language, and Kannada, a Dravidian language, learn to read by recognizing the akṣarə as a whole unit and develop phonemic awareness at a much later stage in their pursuit of literacy. The large body of research data on Kannada amassed by Prakash et al., (1993) and Karanth and Prakash (1999) demonstrate a similar trend.

Children learning to read English, French, German, Greek, Japanese, Chinese, Gujarati, Kannada, Hindi and Oriya, for example, which use different writing systems and scripts, pursue reading acquisition on the basis of the linguistic unit and script topography available to them in their cultural–linguistic ecology. There is no one particular linguistic unit or cognitive process, which is absolutely necessary for reading acquisition. Modeling reading acquisition so far has emphasized the issue of segmentation of words into phonological units, especially, at the level of the phoneme; and it has been guided mainly by the data on children learning to read through the Roman alphabetic script in societies with literate cultural practices. It is generally agreed that some form of phonological awareness or sensitivity is a prerequisite for progress in reading acquisition. The awareness about the different linguistic units involved in word composition (morpheme, syllable, mora or *matra*, phoneme) appears to be associated with reading acquisition as well as the development of the mental dictionary.

The variable "phonological awareness" in current experimental research has been conceptualized and operationalized in a trivial way. The focus needs to be shifted away from the acoustic speech code and re-oriented in terms of phonological and orthographic representations in mental lexicon. The developmental path in reading acquisition needs to be explored in relation to the auditory system and the changes in lexical–semantic–syntactic–cognitive representations and processing. At the moment, phonological awareness is examined only in relation to reading acquisition, that is, as a prerequisite, a consequence, or an interactive product. This will pave the way towards a systematic understanding of dyslexic mechanisms and processes in relation to the neurobiology of cognitive–linguistic development.

Research on developmental dyslexia must look at the failure in reading acquisition in children who are conceived and raised in a culture of poverty and the associated environmental conditions. It simply cannot be that neurocognitive development can be immune to stressful circumstances and environment. The boundary of the cycle of disadvantages needs to be opened to examine its manifestations in different societies at different times.

As for phonological theory and reading acquisition, it must be realized that there are alternative models of syllabic organization which do not consider the association between the nucleus and the coda a natural bond, compared to the nucleus and the onset (Vennemann, 1988). The superior performance of children in recognizing the vc unit in learning to read English may be due to some other factors. It may be that syllabic structure is perceived differently in English, Japanese, Korean, etc. It is suggested that Korean and Japanese prefer "left-branching" syllabic division, while English is better suited to "right-branching" syllable structure (Derwing et al., 1993; Kubozono, 1989). The right-branching syllable division separates the onset (syllable-initial consonant) from the rime (the vowel and the following consonant). For example, in the English word "dog," which is a syllable, the dividing units are /d/ and /og/. The left-branching syllable division of this word would be between /do/ and /g/, that is, between the body and the coda.

Interestingly, the application of *matra* values, either a one half or one *matra*, to short and long consonants, respectively, obviates the need for preference for a particular type of a model of syllable structure. It can be simply stated that a sound segment (v, c) or a sequence of sound segments (cv, ccv, cccv, cvv, ccvv, cccvv) which bears one or two *matra*s can form an *akṣarə*. Consonants before vowels cannot bear *matra* value, as they happen to be short in duration. On the other hand, consonants after vowels (cvc or vc) can be short or long in duration and long consonants bear whole *matra* values: Long consonants after vowels in syllables can be *akṣarə*s. Since *matra* values are determined auditorily, *akṣarə*s may be considered perceptual units.

Finally, exploratory research, which does not follow the logic of experimental control and use of standard statistical analytical tools, can also uncover some interesting trends and insights. Subjects need to be looked at both as processing systems and living organisms in specific living conditions. The implications of these trends and insights can play a crucial role in the formulation of research questions which can be investigated in children learning to read in different cultural–linguistic regions using different writing systems and scripts. There are naturally occurring experimental groups of children, as in children from disadvantaged and advantaged scheduled groups; there are separate public schools for female and male pupils from scheduled groups whose parents reside either in isolated ghettoes or upper-class compounds. The hypothesis regarding the inadequacies in the phonological and orthographic lexical representations in the mental dictionary to account for the problems of these children needs refined experimental research. The issue of the possibility of dyslexia-type aberrations in such children caused by extreme poverty, the toxic environment, and the stigma of the caste system calls for a multidisciplinary research program, which must include neurobehavioral teratology.

Glossary

akṣərə	The orthographic unit in Brāhmī scripts.
anusvara	A nasalization marker, a dot or a small circle.
Astadhyayi	The first classic in phonology by Panini who constructed formulaic rules for Sanskrit.
awareness (phonological/phonemic)	A metalinguistic concept related to the level of sound patterns, specifically in terms of syllables and phonemes.
Brāhmī	A major script developed by ancient Indian language scholars.
caste system	A religiously defined hierarchy of levels which classify individuals in terms of birth and division of labor.
coda	A consonant after the vowel in syllable organization.
declarative memory	A system of long-term memory about information and rules which form domains and networks acquired through learning, not by practice.

dorsal channel	A channel which transmits information from the retinal ganglion cells through the magnocellular pathway to cortical visual processing areas in the lower parietal lobe, known as the "where" system.
Dravidian languages	Languages like Tamil, Malayalam, Telugu, Kannada, Tulu, etc., spoken mainly in south India.
episodic memory	A subsystem of declarative memory related to specific events which occur only once.
fMRI (functional magnetic resonance imaging)	A method used to detect functional activities in specific brain regions. Introduces brief magnetic pulses and measures the associated changes.
kramapatha (krəməpaṭhə)	A rearrangement of the con-tinuous recitation of Vedic text into a new order of *padas*: /ab/bc//cd//de/.
lateral geniculate nucleus	A visual information transmission nucleus in the thalamus.
lexical representation	Abstract representation of word form.
magnocellular pathway	A channel which transmits information fast about "where" through the lateral geniculate nucleus in the thalamus and the primary visual cortex to the adjacent lower parietal lobe.
Mathew effects	Negative effects of poor reading skills upon the development of the reading-related cognitive skills: The poor getting poorer process.
matra	A term used by ancient Indian phoneticians for the primary measure of duration which corresponds with the modern linguistic term "mora."
mental dictionary	The word storage system in the human mind.
neurobehavioral teratology	The study of abnormal neural, cognitive, and behavioral child development related to prenatal environmental damage.
nucleus	The vowel in syllable structure.

occipital lobe	A visual processing cortical region located at the back of the head.
orthographic representation	Abstract coded form of the visual features of the letters in words.
pada	A unit originally referring to the individual words which constituted the Vedic samhita text, that is the continuous text used in recitation. Panini's definition of *pada* included complete noun-forms and verb-forms as well as prefixes and suffixes. The units were marked by specific types of pauses.
Panini	The father of modern linguistic science. Lived in, approximately, 500 B.C., in northwest India.
parietal lobe	A cortical region bordering the temporal and the occipital lobes.
parvocellular pathway	A pathway known as the ventral channel which transmits information from the retinal ganglion cells through the lateral geniculate nucleus in the thalamus and the occipital lobe and ends in the adjacent lower temporal lobe.
PET (positron emission tomography)	A method of observing changes in blood flow in specific brain regions. Measures emission of radioactive particles following injection of labelled metabolites.
planum temporale	A triangular landmark located on the superior surface of the temporal lobe close to the primary auditory cortex.
Pratishakhya	Phonetic manuals providing detailed guidelines regarding articulation in recitation of the Vedas, the earliest extant ancient Indian literary creations.
prestriate cortex / extrastriate cortex	The visual processing areas in the temporal, parietal, and occipital lobes, which receive input from the primary visual area, V1, in the occipital lobe.
primary visual center	A small receptive area in the occipital lobe which receives visual information from the

	visual pathway originating in the retinal ganglion cells.
procedural memory	A system of memory about habits and skills which can be acquired by practice and used automatically.
retinal ganglion cells	Cells in the retina connected to the optic nerve fibres which, in turn, are connected to the lateral geniculate nucleus and the primary visual area in the occipital lobe.
Rgved	The earliest Hindu literary creation, considered primary Veda.
sa, re, ga, ma, pa, dha, ni	The seven notes in Indian classical music.
schwa	The mid-central vowel.
children from scheduled groups	The term used in India to identify disadvantaged lower castes and tribal groups of people for official compensatory programs.
script topography	The spatial organization of the visual features and relations in a given script, that is, the way the horizontal, vertical, and circular lines are joined to form letters or *akṣarəs*.
semantic memory	A subsystem of declarative memory which, unlike episodic memory, deals with domains and schemas of knowledge acquired through learning.
Shakalya	The language scholar who segmented the *samhitapatha* of the *Rgveda* into *padapatha*, a masterpiece of linguistic analysis.
striate cortex	Primary visual cortex called V1 (Broadmann's area 17). So called because it looks like a stripe.
syllable quantity	A property of syllable structure related more with the syllable ending, that is, the presence of consonants. The primary measure of syllable quantity is a short vowel, with or without consonants before it.
varnamala	The systematic arrangement of the sounds of Sanskrit into articulatory phonetic classes.

Vedas	The four earliest ancient Indian literary texts, created orally and also preserved through recitation for centuries. The four Vedas are called Rgveda, Yajurveda, Atharvaveda, and Samaveda.
ventral channel	A channel that transmits information from the retinal cells through the parvocellular pathway to the cortical visual processing areas in the lower temporal lobe, known as the "what" system.
vikruti	A linguistic device which rearranges the segmented *padas* in different sequences.

References and Select Bibliography

Abhyankar, K.V. and G.V. Devasthali (1978). *Veda-Vikruti-Lakshana-Samgraha*. Pune: Bhandarkar Oriental Institute.

Abhyankar, K.V. and J.M. Shukla (1986). *A Dictionary of Sanskrit Grammar*. Baroda: Oriental Institute, M.S. University of Baroda.

Adams, J. (1999). 'On Neurodevelopmental Disorders: Perspectives from Neurobehavioral Teratology.' In H. Tager-Flusberg (ed.), *Neurodevelopmental Disorders*, pp. 451–68. Cambridge: The MIT Press.

Allen, W.S. (1953). *Phonetics in Ancient India*. London: Oxford University Press.

———. (1981). 'The Greek Contribution to the History of Phonetics.' In R.E. Asher and E.J.A. Henderson (eds), *Toward a History of Phonetics*, pp. 115–22. Edinburgh: Edinburgh University Press.

———. (1987). *Vox Graeca: The Pronunciation of Classical Greek*. Cambridge: Cambridge University Press.

Anderson, J.M. and C. Ewen (1987). *Principles of Dependency Phonology*. Cambridge: Cambridge University Press.

Andrade, J. (2001). (ed.). *Working Memory in Perspective*. New York: Taylor and Francis Inc.

Anglin, J.M. (1993). Vocabulary Development: A Morphological Analysis. *Monographs of the Society for Research in Child Development*, 58.

Aslin, R.N. and R.H. Hunt (2001). 'Development, Plasticity, and Learning in the Auditory System.' In C.A. Nelson and M. Luciana (eds), *Handbook of Developmental Cognitive Neuroscience*, pp. 205–20. Cambridge: The MIT Press.

Baddeley, A. (1986). *Working Memory*. Oxford: Oxford University Press.

Badian, N.A. (1984). 'Reading Disability in an Epidemiological Context: Incidence and Environmental Correlates.' *Journal of Learning Disabilities*, 17, 129–36.

Balota, D. (1990). 'The Role of Meaning in Word Recognition.' In D.A. Balota, G.B. Flores d'Arcais, and K. Rayner (eds), *Comprehension Processes in Reading*, pp. 9–31. Hillsdale: Lawrence Erlbaum Associates, Publishers.

Barron, R.W. (1981). 'Development of Visual Word Recognition: A Review.' *Reading Research: Advances in Theory and Practice*, 3, 119–58.

Barron, R.W. and J. Baron (1977). 'How Children Get Meaning from Printed Words.' *Child Development*, 48, 587–94.

Bates, E. (1979). *The Emergence of Symbols: Cognition and Communication in Infancy.* New York: Academic Press.

Bloomfield, M. (1916). *Rgveda Repetitions.* Cambridge: Harvard University Press.

Borsting, E., W. Ridder, K. Dudeck, C. Kelley, L. Matsui and J. Motoyama (1996). 'The Presence of a Magnocellular Defect Depends on the Type of Dyslexia.' *Vision Research*, 36, 1047–53.

Bowers, P.G. and L.B. Swanson (1991). 'Naming Speed Deficits in Reading Disability: Multiple Measures of a Singular Process.' *Journal of Experimental Child Psychology*, 51, 195–219.

Bowey, J.A. and J. Francis (1991). 'Phonological Analysis as a Function of Age and Exposure to Reading Instruction.' *Applied Psycholinguistics*, 12, 91–121.

Bowey, J. and J. Hansen (1994). 'The Development of Orthographic Rimes as Units of Word Recognition.' *Journal of Experimental Child Psychology*, 58, 465–88.

Bradley, L. and P.E. Bryant (1978). 'Difficulties in Auditory Organization as a Possible Cause of Reading Backwardness.' *Nature*, 21, 271, 746.

———. (1983). 'Categorizing Sounds and Learning to Read: A Causal Connection.' *Nature*, 301, 419–21.

Brady, S.A. and D.P. Shankweiler (eds) (1990). *Phonological Processes in Literacy.* Hillsdale: Lawrence Erlbaum Associates, Publishers.

Breitmeyer, B.G. (1989). 'A Visually based Deficit in Specific Reading Disability.' *The Irish Journal of Psychology*, 10, 534–41.

Bryant, P., L. Bradley, M. Maclean and J. Crossland (1989). 'Nursery Rhymes, Phonological Skills, and Reading.' *Journal of Child Language*, 16, 407–28.

Bryant, P.E., M. Maclean and L. Bradley (1990). 'Rhyme, Language, and Children's Reading.' *Applied Psycholinguistics*, 11, 237–52.

Bryson, S.E. and J.F. Werker (1989). 'Toward Understanding the Problem in Severely Disabled Readers Part I: Vowel Errors.' *Applied Psycholinguistics*, 10, 1–12.

Burling, R. (1966). 'The Metrics of Children's Verse: A Cross-linguistic Study.' *American Anthropologist*, 68, 1418–41.

Buser, P. and M. Imbert (1992). *Vision.* Cambridge: The MIT Press.

Campbell, R. (1983). 'Writing Nonwords to Dictation.' *Brain and Language*, 19, 153–78.

Caramazza, A. and A.E. Hillis (1990). 'Levels of Representation, Co-ordinate Frames, and Unilateral Neglect.' *Cognitive Neuropsychology*, 7, 391–445.

Carr, T. and M.I. Posner (1995). 'The Impact of Learning to Read on the Functional Anatomy of Language Processing.' In B. de Gelder and J. Morais (eds), *Speech and Reading*, pp. 267–301. London: Erlbaum (UK) Taylor & Francis.

Carroll, J.B., P. Davies and B. Richman (1971). *Word Frequency Book.* New York: American Heritage Publishing Company.

Chakrabarti, S. (1996). *A Critical Linguistic Study of the Pratishakhyas*. Calcutta: Punthi-Pustak.

Chall, J. S., V.A. Jacobs and L.E. Baldwin (1990). *The Reading Crisis: Why Poor Children Fall Behind*. Cambridge: Harvard University Press.

Chase, C.H. (1996). 'A Visual Deficit Model of Developmental Dyslexia.' In C.H. Chase, G.D. Rosen, and G.F. Sherman (eds), *Developmental Dyslexia: Neural, Cognitive, and Genetic Mechanisms*. Baltimore: York Press.

Chiarello, C. (1991). 'Interpretation of Word Meanings by the Cerebral Hemispheres.' In P.J. Schwanenflugel (ed.), *The Psychology of Word Meanings*. Hillsdale: Lawrence Erlbaum Associates, Publishers.

Clements, E. (1981). *Introduction to the Study of Indian Music*. New Delhi: Gaurav Publications. (Originally published in 1913 by Longmans Green and Co.)

Clifton, C., L. Frazier and K. Rayner (eds) (1994). *Perspectives on Sentence Processing*. Hillsdale: Lawrence Erlbaum Associates, Publishers.

Coleman, E. (1981). 'An Educational Experimental Station for Reading: How can Learning to Read be Facilitated?' *Reading Research: Advances in Theory and Research*, 2, 177–230.

Conners, C.K. (1990). 'Dyslexia and the Neurophysiology of Attention.' In G. Pavlidis (ed.), *Perspectives on Dyslexia*, Volume I, pp. 163–95. New York: John Wiley & Sons.

Coulmas, F. (1996). *The Blackwell Encyclopedia of Writing Systems of the World*. Oxford: Blackwell Publishers.

Cutler, A. and J. Mehler (1993). 'The Periodicity Bias.' *Journal of Phonetics*, 21, 103–08.

Cutting, J.E. (1974). 'Two Left-hemisphere Mechanisms in Speech Perception.' *Perception and Psychophysics*, 16, 601–12.

Dannemiller, J.L. (2001). 'Brain-behavior Relationships in Early Visual Development.' In C.A. Nelson and M. Luciana (eds), *Handbook of Developmental Cognitive Neuroscience*, pp. 221–35. Cambridge: The MIT Press.

Daswani, C.J. (1999). 'Adult Literacy in India: Assumptions and Implications.' In D.A. Wagner, R.L. Venezky, and B.V. Street (eds), *Literacy: An International Handbook*, pp. 434–38. Boulder, Colorado: Westview Press.

Delgutte, B. and N.Y.S. Kiang (1984). 'Speech Coding in the Auditory Nerve IV: Sounds with Consonant-like Dynamic Characteristics.' *Journal of the Acoustical Society of America*, 75, 897–907.

Demb, J.B., G.M. Boynton and D.J. Heeger (1998). 'Functional Magnetic Resonance Imaging of Early Visual Pathways in Dyslexia.' *Journal of Neuroscience*, 18, 39–51.

Derwing, B.L., Y.B. Yoon and S. Whan (1993). 'The Organization of the Korean Syllable: Experimental Evidence.' In P.M. Clancy (ed.), *Japanese/Korean Linguistics*. Stanford: Stanford Linguistics Association.

Deutsch, D. and P. Roll (1976). 'Separate "what" and "where" Decision Mechanism in Processing a Dichotic Tonal Sequence.' *Journal of Experimental Psychology: Human Perception and Performance*, 2, 23–29.

Devasthali, G.V. (1978). 'Kramapatha.' *Annals of the Bhandarkar Oriental Institute* (Diamond Jubilee Volume), 573–82.

Diamond, M. (1988). *Enriching Heredity: The Impact of the Environment on the Anatomy of the Brain*. New York: The Free Press.

Divenyi, P.L. and R. Efron (1979). 'Spectral Versus Temporal Features in Dichotic Listening.' *Brain and Language*, 7, 375–86.

Doehring, D.G. (1976). 'Acquisition of Rapid Reading Responses.' *Monographs of the Society for Research in Child Development*, 41, 165.

Doehring, D.G., R.L. Trites, P.G. Patel and C. Fiedorowitz (1981). *Reading Disabilities: The Interaction of Reading, Language, and Neuropsychological Deficits*. New York: Academic Press.

Dorman, M.F., L.J. Raphael and A.M. Liberman (1979). 'Some Experiments on the Sound of Silence in Phonetic Perception.' *Journal of the Acoustical Society of America*, 65, 1518–32.

Eden, G.F., J.F. Stein, H.M. Wood and F.B. Wood (1995). 'Temporal and Spatial Processing in Reading Disabled and Normal Children.' *Cortex*, 31, 451–68.

Ehri, L.C. (1992). 'Reconceptualizing the Development of Sight Word Reading and its Relationship to Reading.' In P.B. Gough, L.C. Ehri, and R. Treiman (eds), *Reading Acquisition*, pp. 107–43. Hillsdale: Lawrence Erlbaum Associates, Publishers.

———. (1998). 'Grapheme-phoneme Knowledge is Essential for Learning to Read Words in English.' In J.L. Metsala and L.C. Ehri (eds), *Word Recognition in Beginning Literacy*, pp. 3–40. Mahwah: Lawrence Erlbaum Associates, Publishers.

Ehri, L.C. and L.S. Wilce (1983a). 'The Influence of Orthography on Reader's Conceptualization of the Phonemic Structure of Words.' *Applied Psycholinguistics*, 1, 371–85.

———. (1983b). 'Movement into Reading: Is the First Stage of Printed Word Learning Visual or Phonetic?' *Reading Research Quarterly*, 20, 163–79.

Eisenberg, L. (1978). 'Definitions of Dyslexia: Their Consequences for Research and Policy.' In A.L. Benton and D. Pearl (eds), *Dyslexia: An Appraisal of Current Knowledge*, pp. 29–42. New York: Oxford University Press.

Ellis, A.W., A.W. Young and C. Anderson (1988). 'Modes of Word Recognition in the Left and Right Cerebral Hemispheres.' *Brain and Language*, 35, 254–73.

Farmer, M.E. and R.M. Klein (1995). 'The Evidence for a Temporal Processing Deficit Linked to Dyslexia: A Review.' *Psychonomic Bulletin and Review*, 2, 460–93.

Filipek, P.A., Bruce F. Pennington, Jack H. Simon, Christopher M. Filley and John C. DeFries (1999). 'Structural and Functional Neuroanatomy in Reading Disorder.' In D. Duane (ed.), *Reading and Attention Disorders: Neurobiological Correlates*. Baltimore: York Press, Inc.

Fletcher, J.M. and P. Satz (1985). 'Cluster Analysis and the Search for Learning Disability Subtypes.' In B.P. Rourke (ed.), *Neuropsychology of Learning Disabilities*, pp. 40–64. New York: The Guilford Press.

Fletcher, J.M., K.A. Espy, D.J. Francis, K.C. Davidson, B.P. Rourke and S.E. Shaywitz (1989). 'Comparisons of Cutoff and Regression-based Definitions of Reading Disabilities.' *Journal of Learning Disabilities*, 22, 334–55.

Fletcher, J.M., B.R. Foarman, S.E. Shaywitz and B.A. Shaywitz (1999). 'Conceptual and Methodological Issues in Dyslexia Research: A Lesson for Developmental Disorders.' In H. Tager-Flusberg (ed.), *Neurodevelopmental Disorders*, pp. 271–305. Cambridge: The MIT Press.

Fowler, C.A., I.Y. Liberman and D. Shankweiler (1977). 'On Interpreting the Error Pattern in Beginning Reading.' *Language and Speech*, 20, 162–73.

Fowler, C.A., I.Y. Liberman and D. Shankweiler (1979). 'Apprehending Spelling Patterns for Vowels: A Developmental Study.' *Language and Speech*, 22, 243–52.

Fox, B. and D.K. Routh (1975). 'Analyzing Spoken Language into Words, Syllables, and Phonemes: A Developmental Study.' *Journal of Psycholinguistic Research*, 4, 331–42.

Fox Strangways, A.H. (1994). *The Music of Hindostan*. New Delhi: Munshiram Manoharlal Publishers. (Originally published in 1914 by Clarendon Press.)

Galaburda, A. and F. Sanides (1980). 'Cytoarchitectonic Organization of the Human Auditory Cortex.' *Journal of Comparative Neurology*, 190, 597–610.

Galaburda, A.M., M.T. Menard and G.D. Rosen (1994). 'Evidence for Aberrant Auditory Anatomy in Developmental Dyslexia.' *Proceedings of the National Academy of Science USA*, 91, 8010–13.

Golinkoff, R.M. and R.R. Rosinski (1976). 'Decoding, Semantic Processing, and Reading Comprehension Skill.' *Child Development*, 47, 252–58.

Goswami, U. (1998). 'The Role of Analogies in the Development of Word Recognition.' In J.L. Metsala and L.C. Ehri (eds), *Word Recognition in Beginning Literacy*, pp. 41–63. Mahwa: Lawrence Erlbaum Associates, Publishers.

Goswami, U. and P.E. Bryant (1990). *Phonological Skills and Learning to Read*. Hillsdale: Lawrence Erlbaum Associates, Publishers.

Goswami, U., C. Porpodas and S. Wheelwright (1997). 'Children's Orthographic Representations in English and Greek.' *European Journal of Psychology of Education*, 12, 273–92.

Goswami, U., J. Gombert and F. De Barrera (1999). 'Children's Orthographic Representations and Linguistic Transparency: Nonsense Word Reading in English, French and Spanish.' *Applied Psycholinguistics*, 19, 19–52.

Gough, P.B., L. C. Ehri and R. Treiman (eds) (1992). *Reading Acquisition*. Hillsdale: Lawrence Erlbaum Associates, Publishers.

Gough, P.B., C. Juel and P.L. Griffith (1992). 'Reading, Spelling, and the Orthographic Cipher.' In P.B Gough, L.C. Ehri, and R. Treiman (eds), *Reading Acquisition*. Hillsdale: Lawrence Erlbaum Associates, Publishers.

Greenough, W.T. and A.A. Alaantra (1993). 'The Roles of Experience in Different Developmental Information Stage Processes.' In B. de Boysson-Bardies, S. de Schonen, P. Jusczyk, P. McNeilage and J. Morton (eds), *Developmental Neurocognition*, pp. 3–16. Dodrecht: Kluwer Academic Publishers.

Griffith, P. (1986). 'Early Vocabulary.' In P. Fletcher and M. Garman (eds), *Language Acquisition*, pp. 279–306. New York: Cambridge University Press.

Grigorenko, E.L., F.B. Wood, M.S. Meyer, L.A. Hart, W.C. Speed, A. Shuster and D. L. Pauls (1997). 'Susceptibility Loci for Distinct Components of Developmental Dyslexia on Chromosomes 6 and 15.' *American Journal of Human Genetics*, 60, 27–39.

Gupta, S.P. and K.S. Ramachandran (eds) (1979). *The Origin of Brāhmī*. Delhi: D.K. Publications.

Gussmann, E. (2002). *Phonology: Analysis and Theory*. Cambridge: Cambridge University Press.

Heim, S., C. Eulitz, J. Kaufmann, I. Füchter, C. Panter, A. Lamprecht-Dinnesen, P. Matulat, P. Scheer, M. Borstel and T. Elbert (2000). 'Atypical Organization of the Auditory Cortex in Dyslexia as Revealed by MEG.' *Neuropsychologia*, 38, 1749–59.

Helfgott, J.A. (1976). 'Phonemic Segmentation and Blending Skills of Kindergarten Children: Implications for Beginning Reading.' *Contemporary Educational Psychology*, 157–69.

Hirsh, I.J. (1959). 'Auditory Perception of Temporal Order.' *Journal of the Acoustical Society of America*, 3, 157–78.

Hirsh-Pasek, K., D.G. Kemler-Nelson, P.W. Jusczyk, K. Wright-Cassidy, B. Druss and L. Kennedy (1987). 'Clauses are Perceptual Units for Young Infants.' *Cognition*, 26, 269–86.

Horwitz, B., J.M. Rumsey and B.C. Donohue (1998). 'Functional Connectivity of the Angular Gyrus in Normal Reading and Dyslexia.' *Proceedings of the National Academy of Science USA*, 95, 8939–44.

Hutson, K.A. (1997). 'The Ipisilateral Auditory Pathway: A Psychobiological Perspective.' In S. Christman (ed.), *Cerebral Asymmetries in Sensory and Perceptual Processing*, pp. 383–466. New York: Elsevier Science B.V.

Hynd, G.W. and M. Semrud-Clickeman (1989). 'Dyslexia and Neurodevelopmental Pathology: Relationships to Cognition, Intelligence, and Reading Skill Acquisition.' *Journal of Learning Disabilities*, 22, 204–16.

Hynd, G.W., J. Hall, E.S. Novey, D. Eliopulos, K. Black, J.J. Gonzales, J.E. Edmonds, C. Riccio and M. Cohen (1995). 'Dyslexia and Corpus Callosum Morphology.' *Archives of Neurology*, 52, 32–38.

Jha, V.N. (1987). *Studies in the Padapathas and Vedic Philology*. Delhi: Pratibha Prakashan.

Karanth, P. and P. Prakash (1999). *A Developmental Investigation of Onset, Progress and Stages of Literacy Acquisition: Its Implications for Instructional Process*. New Delhi: Department of Educational Research and Policy Perspective, NCERT.

Katada, F. (1990). 'On the Representation of Moras: Evidence from a Language Game.' *Linguistic Inquiry*, 21, 641–46.

Kesavan, B.S. (1988). *History of Printing and Publishing in India: A Story of Cultural Reawakening*. New Delhi: National Book Trust.

Kess, J.F. and T. Miyamoto (1999). *The Japanese Mental Lexicon: Psycholinguistic Studies of Kana and Kanji Processing*. Philadelphia: John Benjamins Publishing Company.

Kintsch, W. (1988). 'The Role of Knowledge in Discourse Comprehension: A Construction-integration Model.' *Psychological Review*, 95, 163–82.

Kiparsky, P. (1979). 'Metrical Structure Assignment is Cyclic.' *Linguistic Inquiry*, 10, 421–41.

Kirshenblatt-Gimblett, B. (ed.) (1976). *Speech Play*. Philadelphia: University of Pennsylvania Press.

Konishi, M. (1995). 'Neural Mechanisms of Auditory Image Formation.' In M. Gazzaniga (ed.), *The Cognitive Neurosciences*, pp. 269–79. Cambridge: The MIT Press.

Kosslyn, S.M. (1987). 'Seeing and Imaging in the Cerebral Hemispheres: A Computation Approach.' *Psychological Review*, 94, 148–75.

Kubozono, H. (1989). 'The Mora and Syllable Structure in Japanese: Evidence from Speech Errors.' *Language and Speech*, 32, 249–78.

Kujala, T., K. Myllyviita, M. Tervaniemi, K. Alho, J. Kallio and J. Näätänen (2000). 'Basic Auditory Dysfunction in Dyslexia as Demonstrated by Brain Activity Measurements.' *Psychophysiology*, 37, 262–66.

Landau, B. (1993). 'Where is What and What's Where: The Language of Objects in Space.' In L.R. Gleitman and B. Landau (eds), *Acquisition of the Lexican*, Special Issue, *Lingua*, 92, 259–96.

Landau, B. and R. Jackendoff (1994). '"What" and "Where" in Spatial Language and Spatial Cognition.' *Behavioral and Brain Sciences*, 16, 217–65.

Larsen, J.P., T. Hoin and H. Odegaard (1992). 'Magnetic Resonance Imaging of the Corpus Callosum in Developmental Dyslexia.' *Cognitive Neuropsychology*, 9, 123–34.

Leiner, H.C., A.L. Leiner and R.S. Dow (1993). 'Cognitive and Language Functions of the Human Cerebellum.' *Trends in Neuroscience*, 16, 444–47.

Lester, B.M. and C.F. Zachariah-Boukydis (eds) (1985). *Infant Crying: Theoretical and Research Perspectives.* New York: Plenum Press.

Levelt, W.J.M. and L.Wheeldon (1995). 'Do Speakers have Access to a Mental Syllabary?' In J. Mehler and S. Franck (eds), *Cognition on Cognition*, pp. 301–31. Cambridge: The MIT Press.

Liberman, I.Y., D. Shankweiler, F.W. Fischer and B. Carter (1974). 'Explicit Syllable and Phoneme Segmentation in the Young Child.' *Journal of Experimental Child Psychology*, 18, 201–12.

Liegeois-Chauvel, C., A. Musolino and P. Chauvel (1991). 'Localization of the Primary Auditory Area in Man.' *Brain*, 114, 139–53.

Livingstone, M.S., G. Rosen, F. Drislane and A. Galaburda (1991). 'Physiological and Anatomical Evidence for a Magnocellular Defect in Developmental Dyslexia.' *Proceedings of the National Academy of Science USA*, 88, 7943–47.

Lovegrove, W., F. Martin and W. Slaghui (1986). 'A Theoretical and Experimental Case for a Visual Deficit in Specific Reading Disability.' *Cognitive Neuropsychology*, 3, 225–67.

Maclean, M., P.E. Bryant and L. Bradley (1987). 'Rhymes, Nursery Rhymes and Reading in Early Childhood.' *Merrill-Palmer Quarterly*, 33, 255–82.

Mahulkar, D.D. (1981). *The Pratishakhya Tradition and Modern Linguistics.* Baroda: The M.S. University Press.

———. (1990). *Pre-Paninian Linguistic Studies.* New Delhi: Northern Book Center.

Mann, V.A. (1986). 'Phonological Awareness: The Role of Reading Experience.' *Cognition*, 24, 65–92.

Marslen-Wilson, W. (ed.) (1989). 'Access and Integration: Projecting Sound onto Meaning.' In W. Marslen-Wilson (ed.), *Lexical Representation and Process*, pp. 3–24. Cambridge: The MIT Press.

Marsolek, C.J., S.M. Kosslyn and L. Squire (1992). 'Form-specific Visual Priming in the Right Cerebral Hemisphere.' *Journal of Experimental Psychology: Learning, Memory, and Cognition*, 18, 492–508.

Mattingly, I.G. (1978). 'The Skills of the Plodder.' *Contemporary Psychology*, 23, 731–32.

Meccacci, L. (1997). 'Temporal Frequency Processing.' In S. Christman (ed.), *Cerebral Asymmetries in Sensory and Perceptual Processing*, pp. 31–54. New York: Elsevier Science B.V.

Metsala, J.L. and A.C. Walley (1998). 'Spoken Vocabulary Growth and the Segmental Restructuring of Lexical Representations: Precursors to Phonemic Awareness and Early Reading Ability.' In J.L Metsala and L.C. Ehri (eds), *Word Recognition in Beginning Literacy*, pp. 89–120. Mahwah: Lawrence Erlbaum Associates, Publishers.

Miller, R. (1967). *The Japanese Language.* Chicago: University of Chicago Press.

Milner, A.D. and M.A. Goodale (1995). *The Visual Brain in Action.* New York: Oxford University Press.

Mistry, P.J. (1996). 'Gujarati Writing.' In P.T. Daniels and W. Bright (eds), *The World's Writing Systems,* pp. 391–94. Oxford: Oxford University Press.

Mohanan, K.P. (1986). *The Theory of Lexical Phonology.* Dodrecht: Reidel.

Monroe, M. (1951). *Growing into Reading: How Readiness for Reading Develops at Home and at School.* New York: Greenwood Press, Publishers.

Morais, J., L. Cary, J. Alegria and P. Bertelson (1979). 'Does Awareness of Speech as a Sequence of Phones Arise Spontaneously?' *Cognition,* 7, 323–31.

Nicolson, R.I. and A.J. Fawcett (1999). 'Developmental Dyslexia: The Role of the Cerebellum.' In I. Lundberg, F.E. Tonneessen, and I. Austad (eds), *Dyslexia: Advances in Theory and Practice,* pp. 173–96. London: Kluwer Academic Publishers.

Olson, R.K., B. Wise, F. Conners, J. Rack and D. Fulker (1989). 'Specific Deficits in Component Reading and Language Skills: Genetic and Environmental Influences.' *Journal of Learning Disabilities,* 22, 339–48.

Olson, R. (2001). Talk given at the Nato Advanced Study Institute on Literacy Development at Il Ciocco.

Oza, G.H. (1918). *Bharatiya Prachin Lipimala.* Delhi: Munshiram Manoharlal.

Parulekar, R.V. (1939). *Literacy in India.* London: Macmillan and Co.

Patel, P.G. (1977a). Review of *Young Fluent Readers* by M. Clark. *Journal of Child Language,* 4, 139–47.

———. (1977b). 'The Left Parieto-Temporo-Occipital Junction, Semantic Aphasia and Language Development around Age Seven.' *Linguistics,* 196, 35–48.

———. (1981). 'Impaired Language Mechanisms in Specific Reading Disability: An Exploratory Synthesis of Research Findings.' *Indian Educational Review,* 16, 46–64.

———. (1983). Review article on *Orthography, Reading, and Dyslexia* (edited by J.F. Kavanagh and R.L. Venezky). *Language,* 59, 636–53.

———. (1995). 'Brāhmī Scripts, Orthographic Units, and Reading Acquisition.' In I. Taylor and D. Olson (eds), *Scripts and Reading : Reading and Learning to Read in the World's Scripts,* pp. 265–75. London: Kluwer Academic Publishers.

———. (1996). 'Linguistic and Cognitive Aspects of the Orality-literacy Complex in Ancient India.' *Language and Communication,* 16, 315–29.

Patel, P.G. and P. Patterson (1982). 'Precocious Reading Acquisition: Psycholinguistic Development, IQ, and Home Background.' *First Language,* 3, 139–53.

Patel, P.G. and H.V. Soper (1987). 'Acquisition of Reading and Spelling in a Syllabophonemic Writing System.' *Language and Speech,* 30, 69–81.

Pereira, A.S. (1999). 'Most Indians do not Read.' *Herald,* XCIX, February 9.

Perfetti, C.A., I. Beck, I. Bell and C. Hughes (1987). 'Phonemic Knowledge and Learning to Read are Reciprocal: A Longitudinal Study of First Grade Children.' *Merrill-Palmer Quarterly,* 33, 283–319.

Perfetti, C.A. and L. Bell (1991). 'Phonemic Activation During the First 40 ms of Word Identification: Evidence from Backward Masking and Priming.' *Journal of Memory and Language,* 30, 473–85.

Perfetti, C.A., L. Bell and S.M. Delaney (1988). 'Automatic (Prelexical) Phonetic Activation in Silent Word Reading: Evidence from Backward Masking.' *Journal of Memory and Language,* 27, 59–70.

Perfetti, C.A. and S. Zhang (1991). 'Phonological Processes in Reading Chinese Characters.' *Journal of Experimental Psychology: Learning, Memory, and Cognition*, 17, 633–43.

Petersen, S.E., P. Fox, A. Snyder and M. Raichle (1990). 'Activation of Extrastriate and Frontal Cortical Areas by Visual Words and Word-like Stimuli.' *Science*, 249, 1041–44.

Phillips, D.P. and M.E. Farmer (1990). 'Acquired Word Deafness and the Time Frame of Processing in the Primary Auditory Cortex.' *Behavioral Brain Research*, 40, 85–94.

Phillips, D.P., R.A. Reale and J.F. Brugge (1991). 'Stimulus Processing in the Auditory Cortex.' In R.A. Altschuler, R. Bonnin, B.M. Clopton, and D.W. Hoffman (eds) (1991), *Neurobiology of Hearing: The Central Auditory System*, pp. 335–65. New York: Raven Press.

Pickles, J.O. (1988). *In Introduction to the Physiology of Hearing*. San Diego: Academic Press.

Pollastek, A., M. Lesch, R. Morris and K. Rayner (1992). 'Phonological Codes are Used in Integrating Information Across Saccades in Word Identification and Reading.' *Journal of Experimental Psychology: Human Perception and Performance*, 18, 148–62.

Popley, H.A. (1986). *The Music of India*. Varanasi: Indological Book House.

Posner, M.I. and B.D. McCandliss (1999). 'Brain Circuitry During Reading.' In R.M. Klein and P. McMullen (eds), *Converging Methods for Understanding Reading and Dyslexia*, pp. 305–37. Cambridge: The MIT Press.

Prakash, P., D. Rekha, R. Nigam and P. Karanth (1993). 'Phonological Awareness, Orthography, and Literacy.' In R.J. Scholes (ed.), *Literacy and Language Analysis*, pp. 55–70. Hillsdale: Lawrence Erlbaum Associates, Publishers.

Priolkar, A.K. (1958). *The Printing Press in India: Its Beginning and Early Development*, Volumes I, II, and III. Bombay: Marathi Samshodhana Mandala.

Pushpa, M. (1981). 'Factors of Social Deprivation Affecting the Primary School Children.' *Indian Educational Review*, 16(2), 1–14.

Rack, J.P., M.J. Snowling and R.K. Olson (1992). 'The Nonword Reading Deficit in Developmental Dyslexia: A Review.' *Reading Research Quarterly*, 27, 29–53.

Rayner, K. and A. Pollatsek (1989). *The Psychology of Reading*. Englewood Cliffs: Prentice-Hall.

Read, C., Zhang Yun-Fei, Nie Hong-Yin and Ding Bao-Qing (1986). 'The Ability to Manipulate Speech Sounds Depends on Knowing Alphabetic Writing.' *Cognition*, 24, 31–44.

Reichle, E.D. and K. Rayner (2002). 'Cognitive Processing and Models of Reading.' In G.K. Hung and K.J. Ciuffreda (eds), *Models of the Visual System*, pp. 565–604. New York: Kluwer Academic/Plenum Publishers.

Reitsma, P. (1983). 'Printed Word Learning in Beginning Readers.' *Journal of Experimental Child Psychology*, 75, 321–39.

Repp, B.H. (1984). 'Can Linguistic Boundaries Change the Effectiveness of Silence as a Phonetic Cue?' *Journal of Phonetics*, 13, 421–31.

Repp, B.H. (1988). 'Integration and Segregation in Speech Perception.' *Language and Speech*, 31, 239–71.

Ribaupierre, F. de (1997). 'Acoustical Information Processing in the Auditory Thalamus and Cerebral Cortex.' In G. Ehret and R. Romand (eds), *The Central Auditory System*, pp. 317–97. Oxford: Oxford University Press.

Rosen, G.D. (1998). 'Animal Models of Developmental Dyslexia: Lessons from Developmental and Cognitive Neuroscience.' In N. Raz (ed.), *The Other Side of the Error Term : Ageing Development as Model Systems in Cognitive Neuroscience*, pp. 53–105. Amsterdam: Elsevier.

Rosner, J. and D.P. Simon (1971). 'The Auditory Analysis Test: An Initial Report.' *Journal of Learning Disabilities*, 4, 384–98.

Rouiller, E.M. (1997). 'Functional Organization of the Auditory Pathways.' In G. Ehret and R. Romand (eds), *The Central Auditory System*, pp. 3–96. Oxford: Oxford University Press.

Rourke, B.P. (ed.) (1985). *Neuropsychology of Learning Disabilities*. New York: The Guilford Press.

Rubin, D.C. (1989). 'Issues of Regularity and Control: Confessions of a Regularity Freak.' In L.W. Poon, D.C. Rubin, and B.A. Wilson (eds), *Everyday Cognition in Adulthood and Late Life*, pp. 84–103. New York: Cambridge University Press.

Rumsey, J.M., M. Casanova, G. Mannheim, N. Patronas, N. Devaughn, S. Hamburger and T. Aquino (1996). 'Corpus Callosum Morphology, as Measured with MRI, in Dyslexic Men.' *Biological Psychiatry*, 39, 769–75.

Rutter, M.L. (1978). 'Prevalence and Types of Dyslexia.' In A.L. Benton and David Pearl (eds), *Dyslexia: An Appraisal of Current Knowledge*, pp. 4–28. New York: Oxford University Press.

Rutter, M.L. and N. Madge (1976). *Cycles of Disadvantage: A Review of Research*. London: Heineman.

Rutter, M.L., J. Tizard and K. Whitmore (1970). *Education, Health and Behaviour*. London: Longman.

Sanches, M. and B. Kirshenblatt-Gimblett (1976). 'Children's Traditional Speech Play and Child Language.' In B. Kirshenblatt-Gimblett (ed.), *Speech Play*, pp. 65–110. Philadelphia: University of Pennsylvania Press.

Scheerer-Neumann, G. (1981). 'The Utilization of Intraword Structure in Poor Readers: Experimental Evidence and a Training Program.' *Psychological Research*, 43, 155–78.

Schmahmann, J.D. (1996). 'From Movement to Thought: Anatomic Substrates of the Cerebeller Contribution to Cognitive Processing.' *Human Brain Mapping*, 4, 174–98.

Seidenberg, M.S., M. Bruck, G. Fornarolo and J. Backman (1985). 'Word Recognition Processes of Poor and Disabled Readers: Do they Necessarily Differ?' *Applied Psycholinguistics*, 6, 161–80.

Shapleske, J., S.L. Rossell, P.W. Woodruff and A.S. David (1999). 'The Planum Temporale: A Systematic, Quantitative Review of its Structural, Functional and Clinical Significance.' *Brain Research Reviews*, 29, 26–49.

Shaywitz, S.E., M.D. Escobar, B.A. Shaywitz, J.M. Fletcher and R. Makuch (1992). 'Evidence that Dyslexia may Represent the Lower Tail of a Normal Distribution of Reading Ability.' *The New England Journal of Medicine*, 326, 145–50.

Shaywitz, S.E., B.A. Shaywitz, K.R. Pugh, R.K. Fulbright, R.T. Constable, W.E. Mencl, D.P. Shankweiler, A.M. Liberman, P. Skudlarski, J.M. Fletcher, L. Katz, K.E. Marchione, C. Lacadie, C. Gatenby and J.C. Gore (1998). 'Functional Disruption in the Organization of the Brain for Reading in Dyslexia.' *Proceedings of the National Academy of Science USA*, 95, 2636–41.

Siegel, L.S. (1988). 'Evidence that IQ Scores are Irrelevant to the Definition and Analysis of Reading Disability.' *Canadian Journal of Psychology*, 42, 202–15.

Siegel, L., D. Share and G. Esther (1995). 'Evidence for Superior Orthographic Skills in Dyslexia.' *Psychological Science*, 6, 250–54.

Slaghui, W.L., W.J. Lovegrove and J.A. Davidson (1993). 'Visual and Language Processing Deficits are Concurrent in Dyslexia.' *Cortex*, 29, 601–15.

Snow, C.E. and C.A. Ferguson (eds) (1977). *Talking to Children: Language Input and Acquisition*. NewYork: Cambridge University Press.

Soderberg, R. (1971). *Reading in Early Childhood: A Linguistic Study of a Swedish Preschool Child's Gradual Acquisition of Reading Ability*. Stockholm: Norstedt.

Spinelli, D., P. Angelelli, M. Deluca, E. DiPace, A. Judica and P. Zoccolotti (1997). 'Developmental Surface Dyslexia is not Associated with Deficits in the Transient Visual System.' *NeuroReport*, 8, 1807–12.

Staal, J.F. (1975). 'The Concept of Metalanguage and its Indian Background.' *Journal of Indian Philosophy*, 3, 315–54.

Stanback, M.L. (1992). 'Syllable and Rime Patterns for Teaching Reading: Analysis of a Frequency-based Vocabulary of 17,602 Words.' *Annals of Dyslexia*, 42, 196–221.

Stanovich, K.E. (1986). 'Mathew Effects in Reading: Some Consequences of Individual Differences in the Acquisition of Literacy.' *Reading Research Quarterly*, 21, 360–407.

———. (1988). 'Explaining the Differences Between the Dyslexic and the Garden-variety Poor Reader: The Phonological–Core–Variable Difference Model.' *Journal of Learning Disabilities*, 21, 590–604.

———. (1991). 'Discrepancy Definitions of Reading Disability: Has Intelligence Led us Astray?' *Reading Research Quarterly*, 26, 1–29.

Stein, J., P. Riddell and S. Flower (1989). 'Disordered Right Hemisphere Function in Developmental Dyslexia.' In C. von Euler, I. Lundberg, and G. Lennerstrand (eds), *Brain and Reading*. New York: Stockton Press.

Stein, J. and V. Walsh (1997). 'To See but Not to Read: The Magnocellular Theory of Dyslexia.' *Trends in Neuroscience*, 20, 147–52.

Steinberg, D.D., Yamada Yun, Nakano Yōko, Hirakāwa Seiko, and Kanemoto Setsuko (1977). 'Meaning and Learning of Kanji and Kana.' *Hiroshima Forum of Psychology*, 4, 15–24.

Stevens, K.N. (1998). *Acoustic Phonetics*. Cambridge: The MIT Press.

Subramanian, C. (1991). 'For a Better Tomorrow.' *Illustrated Weekly of India*, February 2–3, 18–21.

Tallal, P., R.L. Sainburg and T. Jernigan (1991). 'The Neuropathology of Developmental Dysphasia: Behavioural, Morphological, and Physiological Evidence for a Pervasive Temporal Processing Disorder.' *Reading and Writing*, 3, 363–77.

Tallal, P., S. Miller and R.H. Fitch (1993). 'Neurobiological Basis of Speech—A Case for the Pre-eminence of Temporal Processing.' *Annals of the New York Academy of Sciences*, 682, 27–47.

Taylor, I. and D.R. Olson (eds) (1995). *Scripts and Literacy: Reading and Learning to Read Alphabets, Syllabaries and Characters*. London: Kluwer Academic Publishers.

Trehub, S.E. and L.J. Trainor (1993). 'Listening Strategies in Infancy: The Roots of Music and Language Development.' In S. McAdfams and E. Bigand (eds), *Thinking in Sound: Cognitive Aspects of Human Audition*. Oxford: Oxford University Press.

Treiman, R., U. Goswami and M. Bruck (1990). 'Not all Nonwords are Alike: Implications for Reading Development and Theory.' *Memory and Cognition*, 18, 559–67.

Treiman, R., J. Mullennix, R. Bijeljac-Babic and E.D. Richmond-Welty (1995). 'The Special Role of Rimes in the Description, Use and Acquisition of English Orthography.' *Journal of Experimental Psychology*, 124, 107–36.

Trevarthen, C. (1977). 'Descriptive Analyses of Infant Communicative Behavior.' In H.R. Schaffer (ed.), *Studies in Mother-Infant Interaction*, pp. 227–70. London: Academic Press.

Tulving, E. (1985). 'How Many Memory Systems are There?' *American Psychologist*, 40, 385–98.

Upasak, C.S. (1960). *The History and Paleography of Mauryan Brāhmī Script.* Nalanda (Patna): Nava Nalanda Mahavihara.

Varma, S. (1961). *Critical Studies in the Phonetic Observations of Indian Grammarians.* Delhi: Munshiram Manoharlal.

Vasanta, D. (1998). 'Phonological versus Orthographic Coding Strategies in Telugu Deaf Children: Implications for Reading and Spelling Instruction.' In A. Weisel (ed.), *Proceedings of the 18th International Congress on the Education of the Deaf.* Tel Aviv, Israel.

Vennemann, T. (1988). *Preference Laws for Syllable Structure and the Explanation of Sound Change.* Berlin: Mouton de Gruyter.

Verma, T.P. (1971). *The Paleography of Brāhmī Scripts in North India.* Varanasi: Siddharth Prakashan.

Walley, A.C. (1993). 'The Role of Vocabulary Development in Children's Spoken Word Recognition Segmentation Ability.' *Developmental Review*, 13, 286–350.

Walley, A.C. and T.D. Carrell (1983). 'Onset Spectra and Formant Transitions in the Adult's and Child's Perception of Place of Articulation in Stop Consonants.' *Journal of the Acoustical Society of America*, 73, 1011–22.

Weiskrantz, L. (1997). *Consciousness Lost and Found.* Oxford: Oxford University Press.

Werker, J.F., S.E. Bryson and K. Wassenberg (1989). 'Toward Understanding the Problem in Severely Disabled Readers Part II: Consonant Errors.' *Applied Psycholinguistics*, 10, 13–30.

Wolf, M. and M. Obregon (1992). 'Early Naming Deficits, Developmental Dyslexia, and a Specific Deficit Hypothesis.' *Brain and Language*, 42, 219–47.

Wolfenstein, M. (1954). *Children's Humor: A Psychological Analysis.* Glencoe, Ill.: Free Press.

Zatorre, R.J. (1997). 'Hemispheric Specialization of Human Auditory Processing: Perception of Speech and Musical Sounds.' In S. Christman (ed.), *Cerebral Asymmetries in Sensory and Perceptual Processing*, 299–323. New York: Elsevier Science B.V.

Zigmond, M.J., F.E. Bloom, S.C. Landis, J.L. Roberts and L.R. Squire (eds) (1999). *Fundamental Neuroscience.* San Diego: Academic Press.

Zinna, D., I.Y. Liberman and D. Shankweiler (1986). 'Children's Sensitivity to Factors Influencing Vowel Reading.' *Reading Research Quarterly*, 21, 465–80.

Subject Index

Shakalya, 29, 38, 42
sociolinguistic changes, 119, 128
speech games, 22, 37, 52, 53, 54
spiral ganglion cells, 68
Sri Lanka, 26
striate cortex, 69, 71, 72, 135
superior colliculus, 69, 71, 73
superior olivary complex, 68–69
Sylvian fissure, 65, 66

teachers, 98, 99, 102, 110, 112, 115, 123, 126, 145
temporal processing, 74, 89, 134, 141
Tpt, 67
tuition classes, 98

Ubby Dubby, 37, 52, 53

upper-class houses, 136
upper-class residences, 21, 121, 122, 126
upper-class residential compounds, 143, 145, 147

Varnamala, 29, 44–46, 48, 78, 86, 98
Vedas, 38
vikruti, 20, 38–39, 41, 42
vocabulary growth, 51

wedding songs, 53–54
word frequency, 82, 118
word recognition, 51, 61, 64, 70, 76, 78, 80, 86, 128, 136, 140, 145
working memory, 59, 60, 65
writing systems, 31–34, 101, 146, 147

Author Index

About the Author

Purushottam G. Patel has been teaching and pursuing research in linguistics at the University of Ottawa since 1970. He retired as professor from that institution in 1998. Professor Patel's research interests center around the linguistic–neural–cognitive processing system with special attention to reading acquisition and developmental dyslexia. He is, at present, engaged in developing a perspective on the relationship of the Indian Brāhmī script to ancient Indian linguistics and Vedic oral tradition through a phonological analysis. Professor Patel's previous contribution to scholarship includes *Reading Disabilities: The Interaction of Reading, Language, and Neuropsychological Deficits* (co-author), as also several research papers, review articles and book reviews.